WORKBOOK FOR REASONING SKILLS

Exercises for Cognitive Facilitation

SUSAN HOWELL BRUBAKER, M.S., CCC-SP
Speech and Language Pathology
William Beaumont Hospital
Royal Oak, Michigan

Wayne State University Press, Detroit

Copyright © 1983 by Wayne State University Press,
Detroit, Michigan 48202. All rights reserved.
No part of this book may be reproduced without formal
permission.

Second printing, September, 1984

Library of Congress Catalog Card Number 83-50961

ISBN 0-8143-1760-X

To my parents

CONTENTS

Foreword *Michael I. Rolnick*   7
Introduction   8

TARGET AREA 1: DRAWING CONCLUSIONS

Categorizing by Like Attributes   11
Identifying Occupations   16
Identifying Concrete Characteristics   22
Identifying Abstract Characteristics   25
Deciding Appropriate Emotions   30
Ranking by Probability of Outcome   39
Deciding Object Relationships   45
Identifying Familiar Messages   49
Completing Modified Analogies   52
Answering Inferential Questions   55
Categorizing from Descriptions   58
Identifying by Exclusion   63
Identifying Activities from Descriptions   66
Predicting Results from Situations   69
Predicting Situations from Results   75

TARGET AREA 2: PROBLEM SOLVING

Choosing Equipment To Fit Descriptions   85
Determining the Best Alternative   89
Deciding First Steps   95
Thinking Creatively   102
Determining Problems Given Courses of Action   106
Determining Causes Given Results   110
Finding Solutions to Problems   114
Forming Opinions about Current Events   119
Identifying Problems from Solutions   125
Deciding Factors in Making Decisions   130
Determining Pros and Cons   135
Finding Solutions to Multi-Factor Problems   139

TARGET AREA 3: FOLLOWING DIRECTIONS

Following Instructions by Marking Words   147
Recognizing Incorrect Answers   150
Following Unrelated Instructions   153
Decoding If/Then Statements   155
Positioning Letters from Directions   160
Answering Questions with Figures and Symbols   163
Understanding Spatial Relationships   166
Understanding Spatial Directions   168
Drawing by Instruction   172
Locating Information   177
Filling Out Forms   180

TARGET AREA 4: VISUAL/LOGICAL SEQUENCING

Separating Words   185
Tracking Words   188
Respacing Words   190
Answering Alphabet Questions   193
Locating Embedded Words   195
Rearranging Words   198
Ranking by Size   200
Ranking by Attributes   203
Sequencing Steps in a Task   209
Sequencing Informational Statements   213

TARGET AREA 5: HUMOR

Matching Riddles to Answers   221
Solving Riddles   224
Choosing Humorous Answers   228
Completing Jokes   234
Matching Definitions   242
Rewriting Puns   245
Understanding Word Drawings   249

TARGET AREA 6: NUMBERS/SYMBOLS

Matching Symbols and Words   259
Matching Numbers and Facts   261
Identifying Numbers from Descriptions   264
Answering Questions about Quantities   266
Adding Amounts of Money   269
Ranking Costs   271
Identifying Equivalent Values   274
Completing Numbers in a Series   276
Correcting Numbers in a Series   279
Solving Arithmetic Problems   282
Solving Multi-Step Computations   285
Solving Math Story Problems   293

FOREWORD

Effective treatment materials for the rehabilitation of language and cognitive impairment are not always available. Children and adults with brain dysfunction require specifically designed activities that are different from those used by others. This workbook meets the therapeutic needs of that population of individuals who are language-, reasoning-, or cognitively impaired in a comprehensive manner.

Hospitals, schools, and rehabilitation centers are noticing a marked increase in children and adults with varying degrees of brain dysfunction. Survival rates from head injuries in motor vehicle accidents have increased nationwide. More and more stroke and aphasia patients are found in our aging population. Neonatology centers with their sophisticated medical technology can now keep alive many premature infants who would have died only a few years ago. All of these situations contribute to the increasing number of people with identified brain damage.

If we, as rehabilitation workers and educators of the handicapped, are to meet the needs of the people who come to us for help, we must have the necessary tools to provide appropriate intervention. This publication is the third in a series of materials designed to be used for varying degrees of communicative and cognitive dysfunction. Target areas have been carefully chosen to provide exercises which cover most of the aspects of cognitive facilitation that we ordinarily encounter. The exercises range over a wide spectrum. The varying levels of challenge allow for applicability to most types of impairment, making this workbook an extremely valuable aid for the clinician or the educator.

Michael I. Rolnick, Ph.D.
Director, Speech and
Language Pathology Department
William Beaumont Hospital System
Royal Oak, Michigan

INTRODUCTION

This book is the third in a planned series of four workbooks for use with neurologically impaired adults. The first of the series, *Workbook for Aphasia,* included language-oriented activities for the mildly impaired patient. *Sourcebook for Aphasia* was intended for families and provided them with many resources and exercises. It has also proven helpful to clinicians as a source of ideas in their own intervention with speech- and language-impaired children and adults. *Workbook for Reasoning Skills* focuses on activities of cognition—emphasizing logical thinking. The fourth in the series will emphasize language skills, especially as involved with word retrieval and written expression.

The importance of a workbook dealing with reasoning skills is apparent in view of the current emphasis on helping the population with closed-head and right-hemisphere brain damage. Clinicians adapted their materials to fit these clients as the distinction between aphasia therapy and cognitive therapy was recognized. Many activities in the *Workbook for Aphasia* have been found helpful in diagnosing and treating closed-head patients. This new book addresses those needs more directly and expands on certain areas within the same workbook format.

The comments on the earlier books of both speech and language professionals and patients have been most helpful, and many of their suggestions have been incorporated in this volume: for example, some activities have been shortened while the overall variety of activities offered has been increased. The plastic comb binding is also a response to requests. The activities chosen are those which have been successful with patients; which touch on areas not previously published or fully explored, especially in workbook format; or which have been found to be effective in the area of reasoning and thinking skills. The impaired ability of patients to think through ideas, recognize subtleties, interpolate, and conceptualize was a paramount consideration. An awareness of a need for activities in the areas of inductive and deductive thinking, dealing with practical situations, reading comprehension, creative thinking, and the like, was also an important consideration in the preparation of the text.

I chose to make this workbook applicable to persons with some ability to read and write, as I find that they are most stimulated by material appropriate to their age and situation. They also make up a group which often has enough self-direction and motivation to work independently and to derive satisfaction and a sense of accomplishment in so doing.

The ways in which this book is used will of course be highly individualistic. The twenty-two speech and language pathologists on staff at William Beaumont Hospital, for example, find it most beneficial to give patients a personal copy of the book and to assign pages in it over a period of time. The exercises can also be used as stimulus items, as drills for auditory retention or verbal expression, and as a basis for group interaction. The user of the book should note that there may be more than one workable or "right" answer for a question in certain exercises. Allowing the patient to defend his answer logically, in such cases, may also be therapeutic, and a degree of flexibility is important.

Many people are involved in the writing and publication of a book. While the work goes on, life continues to offer the author little surprises and interruptions, regardless of the publisher's deadlines. I am most appreciative to family, friends, and colleagues (I am lucky enough to count my colleagues as friends), who have been integral to the effort here, as in all my publications. My special thanks goes to the staff of Wayne State University Press and to Jean Owen, who, as editor, has done much to ensure the quality of the end result.

Target Area 1
DRAWING CONCLUSIONS

Target Area 1
Drawing Conclusions

Categorizing by Like Attributes

DIRECTIONS: Each item describes something. There are 4 possible things it describes. Circle the word or words that fit the description.
HINT: There may be more than 1 correct answer for each question.

EXAMPLE: They have keys.

(piano)   (hotel clerk)   (typewriter)   speaker

---

1. They have eyes.

   needle   potato   plate   storm

---

2. They have skin.

   oranges   foxes   teeth   trees

---

3. They have more than 2 legs.

   chair   spider   person   stool

---

4. They come from trees.

   walnuts   grapes   sap   apples

5. They climb.

    ivy   light bulbs   monkeys   fish

---

6. They are hot.

    chiles   sun   lava   tin

---

7. They burn.

    wood   aluminum foil   cotton   books

---

8. They are illegal.

    smoking   speeding   kidnapping   leasing

---

9. They have fur.

    people   bears   birds   fish

---

10. They roll.

    marbles   dice   pencils   coins

---

11. They fly.

    flypaper   eagles   jets   flywheels

12. They grow.

    growls   seeds   socks   ferns

---

13. They melt.

    sun   ice   chocolate   paper

---

14. They cut.

    razors   knives   clippers   screws

---

15. They can be spread.

    mayonnaise   onions   paint   light

---

16. They freeze.

    prices   water   alcohol   chicken

---

17. They bounce.

    checks   golf balls   light bulbs   snowballs

18. They are sharp.

    blades   pencil sharpeners   corners   swords

---

19. They can be red.

    onions   books   bananas   traffic lights

---

20. They have nails.

    toes   monkeys   mailbox   toolbox

---

21. They have mouths.

    jars   fish   rivers   shoes

---

22. They have spines.

    porcupines   mattresses   humans   trees

---

23. They have screens.

    ovens   TVs   chairs   windows

---

24. They have bars.

    drums   barbers   jails   restaurants

25. They have trunks.

   elephants   cars   trees   planes

26. They have tails.

   tailors   tuxedos   beavers   kites

27. They contain milk.

   onion soup   ice cream   cocoa   yogurt

28. They have horns.

   toads   cars   goats   hornets

29. They have collars.

   priests   dogs   shirts   collarbones

30. They are plugged in.

   toasters   irons   flashlights   hair dryers

Target Area 1
Drawing Conclusions | Identifying Occupations

DIRECTIONS: Each sentence says something which a certain type of person might say. Choose the person who would be most likely to say it and underline the word.

EXAMPLE: Open wide and say "ah."

    clerk   insurance agent   <u>doctor</u>

---

1. Would you like me to check the oil?

    gas attendant   plumber   telephone operator

---

2. Your flight will leave at 12:30 P.M.

    travel agent   florist   clerk

---

3. We need a written estimate of the damages.

    author   professor   insurance agent

---

4. I promise to help lower the rate of inflation.

    forest ranger   politician   secretary

5. All my friends can stay out until nine, why can't I?

    parent   child   teacher

6. Strike three.

    umpire   pitcher   coach

7. May I take your order?

    chef   receptionist   waitress

8. Roll 'em. . . . That's a take.

    farmer   pilot   director

9. You need a shampoo and a good cut.

    carpenter   hair stylist   editor

10. Love, thirty. Your serve.

    golfer   tennis player   swimmer

11. I've applied for a patent, but I don't have it yet.

    inventor   ballerina   salesperson

12. May I take your blood pressure, please?

   president   actress   nurse

13. Let's try it again with the violins a little louder.

   juggler   harpist   conductor

14. One double scotch, coming right up.

   scientist   bartender   photographer

15. I now pronounce you husband and wife.

   minister   detective   lawyer

16. That will be $10.50 with tax.

   store owner   supervisor   clerk

17. I blocked the damaged artery by performing a bypass.

   surgeon   technician   nurse

18. I can type 70 words a minute.

   explorer   secretary   maid

19. I charge a dollar an hour if I don't have to feed them.

    chauffeur   baby-sitter   yardman

20. Your honor, we have reached a verdict.

    judge   jury   lawyer

21. The paw will be sore for a few days but it should heal fine.

    veterinarian   pediatrician   dentist

22. What sign were you born under?

    astrologer   magician   psychologist

23. There's a short in the line and the main system needs grounding.

    pharmacist   electrician   librarian

24. Your change is $2.03 from $5.00.

    realtor   banker   cashier

25. There's 80 cents postage due on this.

    policeman   mailman   fireman

26. Please fasten your seat belts before takeoff.

    stewardess   travel agent   bellhop

27. Take a cough suppressant and call my office in the morning.

    nurse   doctor   ambulance driver

28. I will be making a mocha torte for 12 today.

    butcher   pastry chef   dietician

29. There's a 12% assumable mortgage available.

    insurance agent   cashier   realtor

30. May I park your car?

    butler   attendant   locksmith

31. I was such an ugly baby the doctor slapped my mother.

    comedian   acrobat   painter

32. Roger to ground control.

    astrologer   astronomer   astronaut

33. Where would you like me to take you?

    chauffeur   choreographer   chimney sweep

34. Would you like the fat trimmed from the roast?

    butcher   banker   barber

35. And now, our top story for the evening.

    cameraman   producer   newscaster

Target Area 1
Drawing Conclusions | Identifying Concrete Characteristics

DIRECTIONS: Circle the word that completes each sentence correctly.

EXAMPLE: A 14-year-old girl is older than a

(12-year-old)   14-year-old boy   24-year-old

---

1. A telephone book is thinner than a

   blanket   pizza   mattress

---

2. A refrigerator is more expensive than a

   car   house   television

---

3. A turtle moves slower than a

   snail   toad   caterpillar

---

4. A fish swims faster than a

   worm   whale   speedboat

---

5. Colorado is farther from Michigan than

   New York   California   Wisconsin

6. A fox is larger than a

    bear   chipmunk   wolf

7. A yardstick is longer than a

    mile   chopstick   sofa

8. A chair is lighter than a

    pillow   record   piano

9. A TV is smaller than a

    motorcycle   microbe   towel

10. A bedspread is harder to carry than a

    pair of skis   bicycle   milk carton

11. A squirrel is tamer than a

    raccoon   tiger   cat

12. Soup that is ready to eat is warmer than

    a 400° oven   tap water   boiling water

13. Wisconsin is farther north than

    Canada   North Carolina   Alaska

14. Arizona is farther west than

    California   Hawaii   Illinois

15. A whistle is louder than a

    train   truck   whisper

16. A splinter is more painful than a

    broken leg   handshake   backrub

17. Crackers are saltier than

    potato chips   cereal   soy sauce

18. A pound of steak is less expensive than a pound of

    lobster   bananas   butter

19. A piece of cheese has more calories than a piece of

    cake   celery   pie

Target Area 1
Drawing Conclusions

Identifying Abstract Characteristics

DIRECTIONS: Put a check in front of the answer to each question.

EXAMPLE: Where would you probably yell?

   _____   at a funeral
   __✓__   at a football game
   _____   at a restaurant
   _____   at a library

---

1. What would probably squeak?

   _____   a small snake
   _____   a baby chipmunk
   _____   a mattress with springs
   _____   a foam mattress

---

2. What would probably smell bad?

   _____   3-week-old fish
   _____   freshly baked cake
   _____   simmering spaghetti sauce
   _____   3-week-old lemons

3. Where would you hear a siren most often?

   _____ on a college campus

   _____ on a lake

   _____ near the woods

   _____ near a hospital

---

4. What would make a dripping sound?

   _____ rain hitting a window

   _____ milk pouring into a glass

   _____ a faucet leaking

   _____ butter melting on a dish

---

5. What would probably make a splash?

   _____ a scarf falling in a pool

   _____ someone diving into a pool

   _____ a cat lapping up milk

   _____ someone wading in a pool

---

6. What sound would be louder than normal?

   _____ a TV tuned to a special news report

   _____ a child using an electric typewriter

   _____ an air conditioner that is running

   _____ a car with a broken muffler

7. What would probably make a whistling sound?

   _____ an angry child

   _____ a boiling teakettle

   _____ dried leaves

   _____ static from a radio

---

8. Where would you probably hear screams?

   _____ near a roller coaster

   _____ near a rose garden

   _____ near a litter of young kittens

   _____ near a bookstore

---

9. What would probably creak?

   _____ a pile of crackers

   _____ leaves rubbing together

   _____ floorboards in a house

   _____ papers being shuffled

---

10. What would probably pop?

    _____ a melting ice cube

    _____ a bag of rocks being shaken

    _____ a champagne bottle being opened

    _____ a sign hanging in the breeze

11. What would probably growl?

    _____ an excited dog

    _____ a bird protecting her young

    _____ a cat playing

    _____ a dog protecting himself

12. Where would you probably hear whispers?

    _____ at a football game

    _____ at a symphony concert

    _____ at a rodeo

    _____ in a cafeteria line

13. Who would you probably hear groan?

    _____ someone going to sleep

    _____ someone in pain

    _____ someone telling a joke

    _____ someone who is blind

14. Where would you probably hear the most crying?

    _____ an amusement park

    _____ a church

    _____ a children's nursery

    _____ a high school

15. Who would you probably hear wheezing?

   _____ someone with asthma
   _____ someone with chicken pox
   _____ someone with herpes
   _____ someone with a charge account

16. Which one would probably be panting?

   _____ a child after waking from a nap
   _____ a man after running 5 miles
   _____ a dog after finishing his dinner
   _____ a woman after typing a letter

17. Where would you probably see the most people?

   _____ at a grocery store
   _____ at a bank
   _____ at a movie theater
   _____ at a football stadium

18. Which situation would make you laugh the most?

   _____ a nightclub act
   _____ a hypnotic trance
   _____ a funeral
   _____ applying for a bank loan

Target Area 1
Drawing Conclusions | Deciding Appropriate Emotions

DIRECTIONS: There are several sentences on each of the next 8 pages. Choose a word from the list at the bottom of each page that best fits the sentence. Write the word under the sentence.

EXAMPLE: The woman paced back and forth across the room and jumped at every sound she heard. She felt

nervous

It hadn't been his idea to go to the concert. He might as well listen since there wasn't anything else for him to do. He felt

bored

nervous   cruel

helpless   bored

A woman said she would go hang gliding but she backed out at the last minute when she realized what she was getting into. She felt

_____

A family was all ready to go on vacation when a last-minute car problem forced them to change their plans. They felt

_____

A woman sat by her phone waiting for a call from her father's doctor. He was rushed to the hospital the day before. She felt

_____

The pitcher pitched a no-hit, no-run game and helped his team win. He felt

_____

A woman took off her glasses and put them on a table. She went into the kitchen, wanted her glasses, but couldn't remember where she put them. She was

_____

afraid	disappointed	happy
absent-minded	envious	ill
brave	generous	worried

A couple was having marital problems. They went to a party where they met 3 other couples who seemed extremely happy and loving. They felt

_____

When a woman heard of a fire that destroyed a friend's apartment, she offered to share her own clothes, meals, and home for as long as needed. She was

_____

A boy could not make up his mind whether he wanted a chocolate bar, popcorn, or jelly beans. He was

_____

The police officer knew the hold-up man had shot another person, but he chased after him in the dark alley anyway. He was

_____

The child's face felt very hot and he had thrown up most of his dinner. He was

_____

afraid	envious	ill
brave	generous	indecisive
disappointed	happy	worried

The little boy pulled the puppy's ears and tail until it squealed. Then he kicked it away. He was

___

The woman looked all through her purse for her keys. Then she realized they were in her coat pocket. She felt

___

They were stuck in the elevator. The problem was being fixed, but in the meantime there was nothing more they could do. They felt

___

The woman was afraid that she was going to faint. The room started spinning and she grabbed for something to hold onto. She felt

___

The cat could smell the tuna fish in the garbage. It couldn't reach it, but somehow it was going to figure out a way to get it. The cat was

___

cruel	enthusiastic	lonely
determined	foolish	nervous
dizzy	helpless	selfish

The cheerleaders smiled and cheered their team. They encouraged the spectators to join them. They were

_____

The salesman told her that learning to use a computer was very simple and that it would pay for itself. She found that hard to believe. She was

_____

Although he knew he should share his new information with the other stockbrokers, he wanted to keep it to himself. He was

_____

It was the singer's first solo. He was perspiring and had butterflies in his stomach. He felt

_____

The elderly man sat and looked around his empty room. He had not had a visitor or phone call for a week. He felt

_____

cruel	foolish	nervous
determined	helpless	selfish
enthusiastic	lonely	skeptical

They smiled as they watched their daughter get her diploma. She had graduated near the top of her class. They felt

_____

He knew he shouldn't have lied. Unfortunately, someone found out and he wished he had told the truth. He felt

_____

The carrot stick slipped out of her hand, and when she tried to pick it up, she spilled her glass of water. She was

_____

He had worked on the same account for 10 hours. He was forgetting things and having trouble focusing. He was

_____

She knew she was spending more time at work than anyone else, but she knew this was the only way to get a promotion. She was

_____

He lifts weights before breakfast, works 9 hours, then jogs 3 miles before dinner and has an active evening. He is

_____

ambitious	clumsy	ignored
ashamed	energetic	proud
bored	hopeful	tired

They had been dating steadily for 6 months. Now she finds out that he has also been seeing someone else. She feels

_____

He didn't know what to do. He knew the fire was spreading. He couldn't go out the door and he was 6 stories up. He felt

_____

She was sitting in the waiting room. There weren't any magazines and she was alone. She had nothing to do. She felt

_____

The 5-year-old was trying to get the adults' attention, but they were busy talking with each other. The child felt

_____

He was divorced, his kids didn't want to see him, his job wasn't going well, and he was behind in his bills. He felt

_____

She gripped the ticket to her heart and closed her eyes. The winner for the big prize was about to be announced and she really wanted to win. She felt

_____

ashamed	hopeful	panic
bored	hurt	proud
depressed	ignored	tired

He's a man of his word. He is _____

His head's in the clouds. He is _____

He's wiped out. He is _____

He's chicken-hearted. He is _____

He's feeling blue. He is _____

He's tickled pink. He is _____

He's climbing the walls. He is _____

daydreaming	nervous	trustworthy
depressed	scared	angry
happy	tired	bored

She's down in the dumps. She is

_____

She needs forty winks. She is

_____

She's got cold feet. She is

_____

She blew her cool. She is

_____

She turned red as a beet. She is

_____

She's pig-headed. She is

_____

She feels like a million dollars. She is

_____

angry	embarrassed	scared
ashamed	happy	stubborn
depressed	lonely	tired

Target Area 1
Drawing Conclusions | Ranking by Probability of Outcome

DIRECTIONS: Each sentence has 5 possible conclusions. One of the 5 is a false conclusion. Mark that answer with an **0** on the line. Of the remaining choices, all might be correct. Number the choices from **1** to **4**. Mark the one that you think is the most likely to occur number **1**. Mark the one you think is next likely number **2**. Mark the next likely number **3**. The one that you think is least likely should be marked number **4**.

EXAMPLE: If someone doesn't eat right

4 he will be overweight.

2 he should take vitamins.

0 it doesn't matter; eating doesn't affect health.

1 he is not getting the proper vitamins and minerals.

3 he should eat more fresh fruit.

REMINDER: 0 - wrong

1 - most likely to occur

2 - next most likely to occur

3 - third most likely to occur

4 - least likely to occur

REMINDER: Mark each question with **0, 1, 2, 3,** and **4.**

1. If a street is paved

    _____ it will last for many years.

    _____ cars will travel faster on it.

    _____ it will have more bumps.

    _____ it will cost the taxpayers money.

    _____ it will have more traffic.

---

2. If a cactus is not watered for a long time

    _____ the dirt will be dry.

    _____ the plant will evaporate.

    _____ the plant may droop.

    _____ the plant will probably survive.

    _____ the plant will probably get a fungus.

---

3. If it rains for 2 days

    _____ there will probably be flooding.

    _____ there might be no food.

    _____ the ground will be dry.

    _____ there might be a power failure.

    _____ outdoor sports will be canceled.

REMINDER: Mark each question with **0, 1, 2, 3,** and **4.**

4. If a grocery store is destroyed by a fire

   _____ food will have to be destroyed.
   _____ it will open the next day as usual.
   _____ arson could be responsible.
   _____ an insurance company will be contacted.
   _____ the store next door will be damaged.

---

5. If a baseball game is rained out

   _____ peanuts and hot dogs are not sold.
   _____ the team plays anyway.
   _____ the players have a day off.
   _____ the game is rescheduled.
   _____ people are mad.

---

6. If a tree is diseased

   _____ the leaves may have holes in them.
   _____ birds that land in it will die.
   _____ it could infect other trees.
   _____ it may be chopped down.
   _____ it loses its leaves.

REMINDER: Mark each question with **0, 1, 2, 3,** and **4.**

7. If someone smokes or drinks too much

   _____ it doesn't matter.

   _____ he will get cancer.

   _____ he doesn't eat properly.

   _____ he bothers others who are around.

   _____ his general health is affected.

---

8. If there is a nuclear war

   _____ no one will be harmed.

   _____ no one will survive.

   _____ it will involve the entire world.

   _____ Russia will start it.

   _____ people will have to evacuate their homes.

---

9. If a company declares bankruptcy

   _____ it has made record profits.

   _____ its credit is poor.

   _____ it owes money.

   _____ it has a cash flow problem.

   _____ it has been managed poorly.

REMINDER: Mark each question with **0, 1, 2, 3,** and **4.**

10. If a couple with young children get a divorce

   _____ the children will be orphans.
   _____ everything will be divided equally.
   _____ the man will pay alimony to the woman.
   _____ they will see a lawyer.
   _____ the woman will move out.

---

11. If a plane is hijacked

   _____ passengers will be frightened.
   _____ the hijacker will demand money.
   _____ the plane will not fly to its planned destination.
   _____ the plane will land safely.
   _____ the pilot will take the passengers as hostages.

---

12. If a man is driving while drunk and is stopped by the police

   _____ he should give the officer a drink.
   _____ he will take a breath test.
   _____ he will be put in jail.
   _____ he will get a ticket.
   _____ he will lose his license.

43

REMINDER: Mark each question with **0, 1, 2, 3,** and **4.**

13. If your freezer breaks down and stops running

    _____ call a repairman.
    _____ your food will thaw.
    _____ your food will spoil.
    _____ it will not affect the food.
    _____ your refrigerator will also stop working.

---

14. If you break a leg

    _____ you will have a cast put on it.
    _____ you will have pain.
    _____ you should have X-rays.
    _____ you should ignore it and walk on it.
    _____ you will use crutches.

---

15. If a person is smuggling drugs into the U.S.

    _____ the government will reward him.
    _____ he will be put in jail.
    _____ he will be caught.
    _____ no one will find out.
    _____ he will make a lot of money.

Target Area 1
Drawing Conclusions
Deciding Object Relationships

DIRECTIONS: The 3 things in each item are related in some way. Think of what they have in common and write it on the line.

EXAMPLE: lens, tripod, film *things to do with photography*

1. garlic, parsley, oregano _____

2. boxes, cartons, drawers _____

3. clippers, polish, emery board _____

4. buttons, snaps, zippers _____

5. Boardwalk, Reading Railroad, Park Place _____

6. Pac-Man, Space Invaders, Donkey Kong _____

7. stem, petals, leaves _____

8. gin rummy, bridge, poker _____

9. lipstick, rouge, mascara _____

10. mustard, onions, ketchup _____

11. tobacco, lighter, filter _____

12. pastels, brush, canvas _____

13. stethoscope, thermometer, tongue depressor _____

14. gills, scales, skin _____

15. craps, roulette, slot machine _____

16. weather, sports, local news _____

17. mane, hooves, bridle _____

18. carburetor, battery, fan belt _____

19. caramel, nougat, chocolate _____

20. innings, fouls, RBIs _____

21. diapers, bibs, strollers _____

22. champagne, confetti, noisemakers _____

23. I.R.S., 1040, April 15 _____

_____

24. chocolate, vanilla, strawberry _____

_____

25. breast stroke, side stroke, crawl _____

_____

26. aisles, cash registers, dairy section _____

_____

27. deposit, withdrawal, accounts _____

_____

28. Bloody Mary, Black Russian, Stinger _____

_____

29. badges, uniforms, nightsticks _____

_____

30. dirt, fertilizer, seed _____

_____

Target Area 1
Drawing Conclusions

Identifying Familiar Messages

DIRECTIONS: You have probably seen all of the phrases listed here many times. Explain briefly next to each message where or when you have seen it.

EXAMPLE: For a limited time only *an ad for a sale*

1. Table of Contents _____

2. Fragile: Handle with Care _____

3. Bake at 350° for 30 minutes _____

4. Exit _____

5. Watch Your Step _____

6. Poison _____

7. No Smoking _____

8. Shake well before using _____

9. No deposit, no return _____

10. In case of emergency, break glass _____

_____

11. Please print _____

12. Slippery When Wet _____

13. Calories per serving _____

14. Box office opens at 5:00 _____

15. For Sale _____

16. Alcohol 13% by volume _____

17. Copyright _____

18. Refrigerate after opening _____

_____

19. Take 2 every 4 hours as needed _____

20. Push _____

21. No Trespassing _____

22. AM, FM _____

23. Close cover before striking _____

24. Machine wash, drip dry _____

25. Coin Return _____

26. Net Deposit _____

27. Caution: Flammable _____

28. We accept Visa or MasterCard _____

29. Beware of the dog _____

30. Please take a number _____

Target Area 1
Drawing Conclusions | Completing Modified Analogies

DIRECTIONS: Each sentence has a blank. Think of a word that makes sense in the sentence, and write it on the line.

The moo of a cow is like the *bark* of a dog.

1. A photographer with his camera is like a painter with his _____.

2. The shell on a nut is like the pod on a _____.

3. The record on a phonograph is like a cassette on a _____.

4. The keys on an organ are like the strings on a _____.

5. The cheese on a pizza is like the frosting on a _____.

6. The cover on a book is like the envelope on a _____.

7. Yarn for knitting is like thread for _____.

8. A seashell on a beach is like a blade of grass on a _____.

9. Sauce for spaghetti is like ketchup for _____.

10. The slithering of a snake is like the hopping of a _____.

11. A hospital for a doctor is like a store for a _____.

12. The upholstery on a sofa is like the _____ on a bed.

13. The lead in a pencil is like the _____ in a pen.

14. The needles on a pine tree are like the _____ on a maple tree.

15. The hand of a person is like the _____ of a dog.

16. Hitting a baseball is like _____ a football.

17. The orange of carrots is like the _____ of tomatoes.

18. The cotton of a shirt is like the _____ of jeans.

19. London in England is like _____ in France.

20. The feathers on a bird are like the _____ on a rabbit.

21. The nose on a face is like the _____ on an elephant.

22. The claws on a chicken are like the _____ on a horse.

23. The handles on a bike are like the _____ on a car.

24. A clerk in a store is like a _____ in a restaurant.

25. Milk in a glass is like _____ in a mug.

26. Flying to a robin is like _____ to a shark.

27. The barking of a dog is like the _____ of a cow.

28. The elbow of your arm is like the _____ of your leg.

29. A bracelet around your wrist is like a _____ around your neck.

30. A house for a person is like the _____ for a snail.

Target Area 1
Drawing Conclusions

Answering Inferential Questions

DIRECTIONS: Write the answer to each question on the line.

EXAMPLE: The ball was hit into the sandtrap. What sport was being played?

golf

1. It's a great day for a picnic. What's the weather like?

2. It picks up peanuts with its trunk. What kind of animal is it?

3. He holds 2 sticks and beats out the rhythm on the skins. What is he playing? _____

4. He got out ice cream and a bowl. What room is he in?

5. He buttons his coat and puts on gloves and a scarf. What is the weather like? _____

6. The car has flashing red lights on top, a siren, a searchlight, and a two-way radio system. What type of car is it?

7. The dry leaves flutter through the air in the wind. What time of year is it? _____

8. After he tightens his skates, he pulls on his face mask, grabs his stick, and takes his place on the ice. What game is he playing?

9. Her eyes are stinging and tears are coming down her cheeks as she chops. What is she chopping? _____

10. A loaf of bread, a jar of jelly, and a box of cereal are on the table. What meal was just eaten? _____

11. She walks from her garage to the back door and reaches into her purse to get something. What is she looking for? _____

12. She puts on an apron, preheats the oven, and takes out a bowl. What is she going to do? _____

13. She rolls the ball and knocks down 8 pins with it. She hopes to get the remaining pins on her second try. What is she doing?

14. The sun beats down on the hot sand. No shade is in sight.

    Where is this? _____

15. He rents a tuxedo for the evening. Where do you think

    he is going? _____

16. When the door opens, 2 people get off and a man gets on. Then

    the door closes and the man pushes the button marked 3.

    Where is he? _____

17. There are many plants and dried flower arrangements around

    you for sale, but you are looking for an orchid. Where are you?

    _____

18. You put the key in the ignition and fasten your seat belt.

    Where are you? _____

19. You are sitting in the stands outdoors with many other people.

    You are watching men in colored uniforms and helmets on a

    field. What are they playing? _____

20. He gets onto the green with a 3-iron shot and 2-putts it into the

    hole. What is he doing? _____

Target Area 1
Drawing Conclusions | Categorizing from Descriptions

DIRECTIONS: Answer each question by writing the answer after it.

EXAMPLE: What looks different when it is wet than when it is dry?

my hair

1. What do you usually do in the winter but not in the summer?

2. What is slippery when it is wet?

3. What do you eat when it is still frozen?

4. What tastes better the day after it has been prepared?

5. What material can you recognize by its feel?

6. What would you do on a rainy day and not on a sunny day?

7. What looks different in different seasons?

8. What do you eat but don't chew?

9. What do people talk to that doesn't talk back?

10. What do you usually buy only once or twice in your life?

11. What job could make you fat?

12. What is less expensive now than it was ten years ago?

13. What takes getting used to when it is new?

14. What is usually too short for tall people?

15. What do you always have more than one of?

16. What can you identify by its smell?

17. What food can you buy frozen or canned?

18. What do you use in the evening and not during the day?

19. What do people often dream about?

20. What would warm you on a cold night?

21. What can change shape?

22. What do you usually keep all your life?

23. What has to be warmed up before you use it?

24. What has a right side and a wrong side?

25. What do you load and unload?

26. What is hard to remember?

27. What should be done very carefully?

28. What can you recognize by its outline?

29. What could you put in the bottom of a grocery bag?

30. What wouldn't you wash with soap and water?

31. What do more men than women do?

32. What do you start but usually do not complete?

33. What do you often do but regret doing later?

34. What is something money cannot buy?

35. What should you avoid if you have a headache?

36. What shouldn't you do if your hands are dirty?

37. What is something people usually don't buy with cash?

38. What should you do very carefully?

Target Area 1
Drawing Conclusions | Identifying by Exclusion

DIRECTIONS: Answer each question in a word or two.

EXAMPLE: What does a maple tree have that a pine tree doesn't have?

It has leaves

1. What can a cat do that a person cannot do?

2. What can a person do that a dog cannot do?

3. What can a waitress do that a customer cannot do?

4. What can a doctor do that a nurse cannot do?

5. What can a computer do that a person cannot do?

6. What can a plow do that a person cannot do?

7. What can a clock do that a watch cannot do?

8. What can our president do that our governor cannot do?

9. What can a turtle do that a fish cannot do?

10. What can a squirrel do that a groundhog cannot do?

11. What can a horse do that a mule cannot do?

12. What can an ant do that an anteater cannot do?

13. What can a judge do that a lawyer cannot do?

14. What can a cow do that a calf cannot do?

65

15. What can Frank Sinatra do that Burt Reynolds cannot do well?

16. What does a kitchen have that a dining room does not have?

17. What does a rosebush have that a hedge does not have?

18. What does college have that high school does not have?

19. What does a peach have that a banana does not have?

20. What does a Cadillac have that a jeep does not have?

21. What does a stew have that a steak does not have?

22. What does a city have that a small town does not have?

Target Area 1
Drawing Conclusions | Identifying Activities from Descriptions

DIRECTIONS: Each item describes an activity. Decide what is being described, and write the name of the activity on the line.

EXAMPLE: Squeeze the white substance on the implement. Place it in the mouth and move it in a circular fashion. What is being done?

brushing your teeth

1. She strikes different keys with her fingers to form words. As she strikes them, she can look up at the paper and see if she has hit the correct letter. What is she doing?

2. He opens the top and begins putting in the items he will need for his trip. These include underwear, socks, and shirts. Then he closes the top to lock it. What is he doing?

3. She puts the key into its holder and presses her foot on the accelerator as she moves the key to a different position. She releases her foot when she hears it catch. What is she doing?

4. She hears a buzzer and a card appears from a machine. After she takes the card, a gate in front of her is lifted. She goes through the gate and it lowers behind her. Where is she?

5. He props the implement under his chin and supports the end of it with his left hand. With his right hand, he holds the bow and gently moves it over the strings. What is he doing?

6. She puts a scoop into a bowl. Then she pours a small amount of dark brown liquid on top of the white scoop in the bowl. She adds some tiny brown chopped bits and tops them with a small shiny red ball. What is she doing?

7. He looks into the eyes of the young thing facing him. Firmly he says, "Sit." He watches hoping the back legs will bend and the rear end will touch the ground. What is he doing?

8. She looks at the piece of cardboard in front of her. She takes a round blue object from the table and begins to look for a certain number under a column marked "N." When she finds it, she places the blue marker over it and listens for the next number. What is she doing?

9. He looks at the canvas in front of him. He looks ahead at the vase of flowers. He sticks a long utensil into a small pot of red. He lifts the utensil out and very carefully begins to transfer the red to the canvas. What is he doing?

10. She walks down the aisle to a row she likes. She moves into the row and sits down. The lights go out, and she looks straight ahead at the large white screen. What is she doing?

_____

11. He is sitting on the grass. With a tool he makes a hole in the brown surface in front of him. He reaches into a small packet and pulls out a small white thing and places it in the hole. Then he fills up the hole. What is he doing?

_____

12. She mixes the thick liquid on her head. Soon it becomes white and bubbly. She continues to mix it into her scalp with her fingers. Then she lets warm water pour over her entire head so that the white mixture begins to disappear. What is she doing?

_____

13. He is sitting on a seat. Ahead of him are two handles which he grasps, one with his left and one with his right hand. They will help him keep his balance on the two wheels as his feet rest on pedals and move round in small circles. What is he doing?

_____

14. She takes the round flat disk out of its jacket and places it on the turntable. Then she turns the machine on, and an arm with a needle moves over the disk. What is she doing?

_____

Target Area 1
Drawing Conclusions | Predicting Results from Situations

DIRECTIONS: Answer each question as completely as possible.

EXAMPLE: What can happen if you do not brush your teeth after every meal?

You can get cavities

1. What can happen if you forget to water plants for a week?

2. What can happen if you do not lock your door when leaving home?

3. What can happen if you do not stop for a red light?

4. What can happen if you do not pay your state taxes?

5. What can happen if you do not rescue a cat from the middle of the street?

6. What can happen if you do not pay your electric bill?

7. What can happen if you do not get a tetanus shot after stepping on a nail?

8. What can happen if you do not wear ear plugs when you are in a very noisy place for a long time?

9. What can happen if you do not repair a leaky pipe?

10. What can happen if you do not get enough sleep?

11. What can happen if you do not take care of a sprained ankle?

12. What can happen if you do not turn off a burner on the stove before you leave the kitchen?

13. What can happen if you do not fill up a gas tank when it says empty?

14. What can happen if you do not examine merchandise carefully before you buy it?

15. What can happen if you do not have car insurance?

16. What can happen if you do not have a credit rating?

17. What can happen if you do not hear an oven timer go off?

18. What can happen if you do not try on clothes in a store before you buy them?

19. What can happen if you do not cook pork until it is well done?

20. What can happen if you do not get a warranty on a product you buy?

21. What can happen if you do not have a spare tire in your car?

22. What can happen if you do not arrive on time for an appointment?

23. What can happen if you do not control your temper?

24. What can happen if you do not explain why you will not be at work on a certain day?

25. What can happen if you do not put out a fire in the fireplace before you go to bed?

26. What can happen if you do not check food for mold before you eat it?

27. What can happen if you do not turn your car lights off when you park?

28. What can happen if you do not clean up a spill on the rug right away?

29. What can happen if you do not chew your food well before you swallow it?

Target Area 1
Drawing Conclusions

Predicting Situations from Results

75

DIRECTIONS: Assume that someone made each statement. Decide what caused the person to say this, and write the explanation on the line.

EXAMPLE: This radio needs a new battery.

The radio wouldn't work when it was turned on.

1. The storm must have been very bad in this area.

_____

_____

2. I'm going to cover the vegetables in the garden tonight.

_____

_____

3. That tree is going to die soon.

_____

_____

4. The bugs must have been eating these tomatoes.

_____

5. That dog is very old.

6. This baby must be very tired.

7. The chicken is not cooked yet.

8. These crackers are stale.

9. The grocery bag was packed poorly.

10. The cheese is spoiled.

11. The roses should bloom in a few weeks.

12. The carpet needs vacuuming.

13. The beer is flat.

14. That person is from the Deep South.

15. He must have sprained his ankle.

16. It is almost quitting time in the office.

17. I think we have a flat tire.

18. The plant needs watering.

19. The man talking to the clerk is angry.

20. Something is burning.

21. The soup is too hot to sip.

22. This knife needs sharpening.

23. I'll be leaving work on time, but I'll be getting home late.

24. Her plane just arrived.

25. I can tell from here that the store is closed.

26. That person should get a ticket.

27. Our neighbor must be out of town.

28. Those workers must be on strike.

29. You sound as though you have a cold.

30. The air conditioner needs to be fixed.

31. The freezer needs defrosting.

32. He's in a bad mood this week.

33. I will need my sunglasses today.

34. My house has been ransacked.

35. Someone must be at the door.

36. The hem needs to be redone.

37. This peach isn't ripe.

38. She must have run all the way home.

39. Someone must have hit the car.

40. You need some stitches in that finger.

41. I'll have to take another picture.

42. There must be a party at their house.

43. That child must be lost.

44. I'd better write down their new address.

45. I need a haircut.

Target Area 2
PROBLEM SOLVING

Target Area 2
Problem Solving
Choosing Equipment To Fit Descriptions

DIRECTIONS: Each sentence is incomplete. Choose one of the words below it that best fits the sentence. Circle that word.

EXAMPLE: If you were taking a temperature, you would need a

    ruler   (thermometer)   pen   glass

---

1. If you wanted to make a piece of felt stick to some wood, you would need

    water   glue   string   Scotch tape

---

2. If you were mending a page torn from a book, you would need

    tape   twine   gum   rope

---

3. If you were installing a door, you would need

    tacks   hinges   scissors   wire

---

4. If you were digging a hole, you would need a

    hammer   yardstick   shovel   rake

5. If you were changing a tire, you would need a

    spark plug   cable   tow truck   jack

---

6. If you were camping in the woods, you would need a

    sleeping bag   reservation   TV   hair dryer

---

7. If you were making tea, you would need

    dirt   plates   coffee   water

---

8. If you were making a cheese sandwich, you would need

    salt   bacon   jam   bread

---

9. If you were taking a photograph, you would need a

    ruler   frame   brush   camera

---

10. If you were unlocking a door, you would need a

    padlock   key   chain   screwdriver

11. If you were cutting the grass, you would need a

    scissors   knife   lawnmower   blade

12. If you were wrapping a gift, you would need

    glue   ribbon   paint   newspaper

13. If you were playing poker, you would need

    nuts   cues   chips   pieces

14. If you were washing clothes, you would need

    wax   detergent   iron   dryer

15. If you were storing leftover food, you would need

    towels   bags   newspapers   foil

16. If you were making French toast, you would need

    garlic   eggs   cheese   bacon

17. If you were knitting a scarf, you would need

    needles   cotton   thread   spools

---

18. If you were tying a boat to a dock, you would need

    rope   string   thread   ribbon

---

19. If you were putting up wallpaper, you would need

    putty   paint   paste   plaster

---

20. If you were planting flowers, you would need a

    hammer   trowel   carton   flashlight

Target Area 2
Problem Solving | Determining the Best Alternative

DIRECTIONS: Each sentence poses a problem. A choice of 4 solutions is given below it. All of the solutions may be possible, but one of them is the best one for the situation. Put a check in front of the **best** solution.

EXAMPLE: If you spill something on the floor, the **best** thing to do is

    _____ lick it up.

    ✓ wipe it up.

    _____ put a rug over it.

    _____ scrape it on a plate and eat it.

---

1. If you need to reach something on a very high shelf, the **best** thing to do is

   _____ stack books on a chair and climb up.

   _____ use a broom to knock it down.

   _____ stand on someone's shoulders.

   _____ stand on a stool.

---

2. When you take a bath, the **best** thing to do is

   _____ take a radio in the tub with you.

   _____ jump in all at once.

   _____ get in, then turn on the hot water.

   _____ feel the water temperature before you get in.

3. If a bad storm is predicted, the **best** thing to do is

   _____ plan an outdoor event.
   _____ stock up on extra food.
   _____ sue the weatherman.
   _____ close the windows.

---

4. If you are driving on a street with potholes, the **best** thing to do is

   _____ speed up.
   _____ slow down and drive over each one.
   _____ slow down and avoid all of them.
   _____ get out and fix them.

---

5. If you are going on a trip for a week, the **best** thing to do is

   _____ give the plants extra water.
   _____ leave the doors unlocked.
   _____ leave the dog in the house for protection.
   _____ do not tell anyone where you are going.

---

6. If you see someone choking on a piece of food, the **best** thing to do is

   _____ laugh.
   _____ ask how it happened.
   _____ hit him on the back.
   _____ nothing.

7. If you are in a strange town and lose your way, the **best** thing to do is

   _____ consult a map.
   _____ keep going.
   _____ ask for directions at a gas station.
   _____ go back home the way you came.

---

8. If you find an injured squirrel, the **best** thing to do is

   _____ pick it up and take it inside.
   _____ find a dog or cat to scare it away.
   _____ call the Humane Society.
   _____ pretend you didn't see it.

---

9. If you think you are getting the flu, the **best** thing to do is

   _____ eat right and get plenty of sleep.
   _____ kiss everyone you can find.
   _____ work overtime.
   _____ check into a hospital.

---

10. If you buy a defective toaster, the **best** thing to do is

    _____ return it to the store.
    _____ sell it to a relative.
    _____ advertise it in the paper.
    _____ throw it out.

11. If airport security people ask to check your bag, the **best** thing to do is

      _____ leave it with them and walk out.

      _____ refuse.

      _____ give it to them.

      _____ panic.

---

12. If you are driving and you see an ambulance coming, the **best** thing to do is

      _____ make sure you are in the center lane of traffic.

      _____ speed up.

      _____ honk and wave.

      _____ pull over to the side of the road.

---

13. If you fall on a slippery floor, the **best** thing to do is

      _____ call a lawyer.

      _____ get up carefully.

      _____ jump up and exercise.

      _____ sit there.

14. If you drop a glass on a wooden floor and it breaks, the **best** thing to do is

   _____ pick up each piece by hand.

   _____ get a broom and dustpan.

   _____ call a child to help clean it up.

   _____ leave it for someone else to take care of.

---

15. If you are walking and find a fallen power line in your path, the **best** thing to do is

   _____ pick it up and move it out of the way.

   _____ call the fire department or power company.

   _____ kick it out of the way.

   _____ call the local news station.

---

16. If you get several harrassing phone calls, the **best** thing to do is

   _____ call the phone company.

   _____ have a conversation with the caller.

   _____ give the caller a friend's number.

   _____ hang up.

17. If you check the water in the bathtub and it is too hot, the **best** thing to do is

   _____ add hot water.

   _____ unplug it and start over.

   _____ add cold water.

   _____ take a shower.

---

18. If you cut your finger with a knife, the **best** thing to do is

   _____ call an ambulance.

   _____ put it down at your side and let it bleed.

   _____ rub soap in it, then put a rubber band around it.

   _____ run cold water on it and then wrap it tightly.

---

19. If you have a toothache, the **best** thing to do is

   _____ get the tooth pulled.

   _____ ignore it.

   _____ eat cold foods.

   _____ call your dentist.

Target Area 2 | Deciding
Problem Solving | First Steps

DIRECTIONS: Each question describes a situation. A choice of actions is given below it. All of the actions may be possible, but one of them should be done first. Put a check in front of the thing which should be done **first.**

EXAMPLE: If you take off your coat and find you are missing a glove, what is the **first** thing to do?

    ✓   Look on the floor near you.

    ___   Visit the checkroom.

    ___   Call the store where you were and report it.

    ___   Buy a new pair of gloves.

---

1. If you wake up with indigestion, what is the **first** thing to do?

    ___ Go back to sleep.

    ___ Do exercises.

    ___ Take an antacid.

    ___ Take your temperature.

---

2. If you accidentally take double the proper dose of medication, what is the **first** thing to do?

    ___ Drink lots of water.

    ___ Call your doctor.

    ___ Call a pharmacist.

    ___ Look at the label to see if it has instructions.

3. If someone comes up behind you and says, "Give me all your money and then hands up," what is the **first** thing to do?

   _____ Scream.

   _____ Turn around.

   _____ Put your hands up.

   _____ Hand over your wallet.

---

4. If a pot on the stove catches on fire, what is the **first** thing to do?

   _____ Call the fire department.

   _____ Pour water or baking soda on it.

   _____ Call a neighbor for help.

   _____ Leave the house.

---

5. If you are driving and see flashing lights in your rear-view mirror, what is the **first** thing to do?

   _____ Check your speed.

   _____ Get out your license.

   _____ Speed up.

   _____ Pull over to the right side of the road.

6. If your keys are not in the pocket you usually keep them in, what is the **first** thing to do?

   _____ Get another set of keys.

   _____ Look in a wastepaper basket.

   _____ Look in another pocket.

   _____ Ask if anyone has seen them.

---

7. If you see a lighted cigarette fall to the carpet, what is the **first** thing to do?

   _____ Find an ashtray.

   _____ Pick it up.

   _____ Grind it out in the carpet.

   _____ Tell off the person who dropped it.

---

8. If you discover a leak under your sink, what is the **first** thing to do?

   _____ Call a plumber.

   _____ Get a bucket.

   _____ Get a pair of pliers.

   _____ Make sure the water is off.

9. If you get stuck in an elevator, what is the **first** thing to do?

   _____ Scream loudly for help.

   _____ Get angry.

   _____ Press the emergency button.

   _____ Faint.

---

10. If you run out of flour in the middle of making a cake, what is the **first** thing to do?

    _____ See if you have another bag of it.

    _____ Substitute sugar for it in the recipe.

    _____ Borrow some from a neighbor.

    _____ Go to the store and buy some more.

---

11. If you are in a store and you can't find your 5-year-old child, what is the **first** thing to do?

    _____ Call out his or her name.

    _____ Telephone your husband or wife.

    _____ Inform the manager of the store.

    _____ Assume the child will return soon.

12. If it is evening and your electricity goes off, what is the **first** thing to do?

   _____ Go to bed.

   _____ Find a flashlight.

   _____ Light a candle.

   _____ Check the houses near you.

---

13. If you find a stray dog, what is the **first** thing to do?

   _____ Feed it.

   _____ Ask your neighbors if they know where it lives.

   _____ Call the dog catcher.

   _____ Check its collar for identification.

---

14. If you arrive late for a job interview, what is the **first** thing to do?

   _____ Pretend you are on time.

   _____ Go to the restroom.

   _____ Apologize and explain why you were late.

   _____ Act defensive.

15. If you see a hit-and-run accident, what is the **first** thing to do?

   _____ Leave the scene of the accident.
   _____ Try to help the victim.
   _____ Call the police.
   _____ Try to recall the license plate of the car.

16. If you feel as though you are going to faint, what is the **first** thing to do?

   _____ Pretend you feel fine.
   _____ Sit down.
   _____ Start running.
   _____ Close your eyes.

17. If you are reading a book and the phone rings, what is the **first** thing to do?

   _____ Mark your place in the book.
   _____ Answer the phone.
   _____ Finish the paragraph you are reading.
   _____ Throw the book at the phone.

18. If you are driving and you think you have a flat tire, what is the **first** thing to do?

    _____ Get out the jack and the spare tire.

    _____ Pull onto the side of the road.

    _____ Speed up to try to make it to your destination.

    _____ Stop as fast as you can where you are.

19. If you are at home and you are too warm, what is the **first** thing to do?

    _____ Have a cold drink.

    _____ Go outside.

    _____ Turn on the air conditioner.

    _____ Take off a sweater.

20. If you burn a casserole, what is the **first** thing to do?

    _____ Turn off the oven.

    _____ Scrape off the burned part.

    _____ Cook it a little longer.

    _____ Throw it out.

Target Area 2
Problem Solving | Thinking Creatively

DIRECTIONS: Answer each question as completely as possible.

EXAMPLE: What can you do with a glass besides drink from it?

You can put water and flowers in it and use it for a vase.

1. What can you do with an old shirt besides wear it?

2. What can you do with a toothpick besides clean your teeth?

3. What can you do with glue besides paste paper together?

4. What can you do with a plastic milk container after it is empty?

5. What can you do with leftover vegetables besides throw them out?

6. What can you do with yarn besides knit with it?

7. What can you do with a wastebasket besides put trash in it?

8. What can you do with a phone book besides look up numbers?

9. What can you do with a paper towel besides dry your hands?

10. What can you do with a basket besides put fruit in it?

11. What can you do with an empty box besides throw it out?

12. What can you do with string besides tie up a package?

13. What can you do with a ball besides bounce it?

14. What can you do with a piece of paper besides write on it?

15. What can you do with butter besides put it on bread?

16. What can you do with chocolate sauce besides put it on ice cream?

17. What can you do with Scotch tape besides mend a torn page with it?

18. What can you do with a tissue besides blow your nose with it?

19. What can you do with chalk besides write on a blackboard?

20. What can you do with rice besides eat it?

21. What can you do with an empty tin can besides throw it out?

22. What can you do with popcorn besides eat it?

Target Area 2
Problem Solving | Determining Problems Given Courses of Action

DIRECTIONS: Answer each question as completely as possible.

EXAMPLE: Why would someone need a vacation?

He has been working very hard and hasn't gotten any time to relax.

1. Why would someone need a respirator?

2. Why would someone need a car battery?

3. Why would someone need an air mattress?

4. Why would someone need an eraser?

5. Why would someone need crutches?

6. Why would someone cough?

7. Why would someone buy a life insurance policy?

8. Why would someone take vitamins?

9. Why would someone use a dictionary?

10. Why would someone buy a cassette tape?

11. Why would someone go on a diet?

12. Why would someone apply for a bank loan?

13. Why would someone need a leash?

14. Why would someone look for a job?

15. Why would someone buy a jumper cable?

16. Why would someone need therapy?

17. Why would someone wear gloves?

18. Why would someone go to an audition?

19. Why would someone hire an attorney?

20. Why would someone want a computer?

21. Why would someone use a microphone?

22. Why would someone wear a veil?

Target Area 2
Problem Solving | Determining Causes Given Results

DIRECTIONS: Answer each question as completely as possible.

EXAMPLE: What could happen to make a lamp fall off a table?

It could be knocked over by someone who bumps into the table.

1. What could happen to cause someone to be on crutches?

2. What could happen to cause a cake to burn?

3. What could happen to cause a shirt to be stained?

4. What could happen to make a letter be returned to you?

5. What could happen to make a squash rot?

6. What could happen to make wallpaper tear?

7. What could happen to make a record skip?

8. What could happen to make a baby cry?

9. What could happen to cause an insurance policy to be cancelled?

10. What could make a dog bark?

11. What could happen to cause a glass to crack?

12. What could happen to cause paint to peel?

13. What could happen to cause a tree to die?

14. What could happen to cause an ice cube to melt?

15. What could happen to cause a balloon to lose air?

16. What could happen to cause someone to be laid off from a job?

17. What could happen to cause a bus to break down?

18. What could happen to cause a boat to sink?

19. What could happen to cause wax to melt on a table?

20. What could cause someone to try to commit suicide?

21. What could happen to make a curtain fade?

22. What could happen to cause a plane flight to be delayed?

Target Area 2
Problem Solving | Finding Solutions to Problems

DIRECTIONS: Each item describes a situation in which you might find yourself. Decide what to do in each case, and write the action on the lines.

EXAMPLE: You are in a library. You want to find the book *War and Peace*. What do you do?

I look it up in the card catalog, then go where the card says.

1. You are taking a bus and want to know where it is going. How do you find out?

2. You are in a clothing store and want to know where the neckties are. How do you locate them?

3. Your eyes hurt. What can you do to make them feel better?

4. You pick up your telephone and the line is dead. What can you do to get it repaired?

5. Your dog is not eating and seems tired all the time. You wonder whether he is really sick. How can you find out?

6. You hear about a store that has something that you want on sale. You don't know where the store is. How can you get the address?

7. You need a lawyer to help you make out a will. You do not know one. How can you find a good lawyer?

8. A hair stylist gave you a $60 permanent wave last week which didn't take. You want another permanent or your money back. What do you do?

9. You have broken out in hives. What do you do?

10. You are to meet someone coming here on a visit. How can you find out if the person's plane will be arriving on time?

11. You think you would like to donate some money to cancer research. How do you find out where to send it?

12. A member of your family finds out that he has diabetes. You don't know much about it. How can you get information?

13. You feel like having fresh scallops. How can you find out whether your local store will have any today?

14. You burn a casserole you were going to serve for dinner, and your guests are due shortly. What can you do?

15. You dent the fender of the car next to you while pulling out of a parking space. What do you do?

16. You are going to visit a building three blocks away. When you step outside, it is raining hard, and you don't have an umbrella. What do you do?

17. You need to know the shortest route from one place to another. How can you find out?

18. You are a U.S. citizen and want to travel to Canada for a vacation. How can you find out about customs regulations?

19. During the night there is a heavy rainstorm in your area. In the morning you discover about an inch of smelly water in your basement. What do you do?

_____

_____

20. It is winter, and your home is very dry. Almost every time you touch something, you see a spark and get an electrical shock. What can you do to prevent this?

_____

_____

21. You are standing in the check-out line at a drugstore. Suddenly you feel dizzy and light-headed. You have a funny feeling going through your body. What do you do?

_____

_____

22. You are on a camping trip for 2 weeks. You are eating corn on the cob around your campfire, and you bite down hard on something. You realize it is a piece of your tooth that has chipped. What do you do?

_____

_____

Target Area 2
Problem Solving | Forming Opinions about Current Events

DIRECTIONS: Each question asks about a current problem. Answer as completely as possible, giving your own ideas on the subject.

EXAMPLE: What could be done to help starving people?

Places which have extra food could give it to those who need it.

1. What could be done to control inflation?

2. What could be done to prevent car accidents involving drunk drivers?

3. What could be done to ensure that taxpayers do not cheat on their income taxes?

4. What do you think is the world's biggest problem, and what could be done about it?

5. What could be done to prevent medicines from being contaminated with poison before people buy them?

6. What could be done to decrease shoplifting?

7. What could be done to get quality programs on TV?

8. What could be done to lower the national debt?

9. What could be done to employ more people?

10. What could be done to cut down home burglaries?

11. What could be done to make sure that the Social Security fund does not run out?

12. What could be done to increase the fuel efficiency of American cars?

13. What could be done to prevent people from getting stuck with a faulty product?

14. What could be done to rehabilitate people in jail?

15. What could be done to prevent unwanted pregnancies?

16. What could be done to find a cure for cancer?

17. What could be done to help children get a better education?

18. What could be done to see that everyone gets a fair trial?

19. What could be done to lessen racial tension in the U.S.?

20. What could be done to prevent mind control by cults?

21. What could be done to prevent smuggling of drugs into the country?

22. What could be done to reduce alcoholism?

23. What could be done to improve relations with Russia?

24. What could be done to prevent vandalism in public buildings?

25. What could be done to prevent overpopulation of animals?

26. What could be done to prevent rape?

27. What could be done to bring about world peace?

28. What could be done to keep peace in the Middle East?

29. What could be done to solve overcrowding in prisons?

125

Target Area 2
Problem Solving
Identifying Problems from Solutions

DIRECTIONS: Each item gives a solution to some type of problem. Decide what problem would require that solution. Write a sentence describing the problem.

EXAMPLE: **Solution:**   Wipe it up with a damp sponge.

Problem: *You spilled some milk on the counter.*

1. **Solution:** Put a bandage on it.

   Problem: _____

2. **Solution:** Vacuum it up.

   Problem: _____

3. **Solution:** Add more salt.

   Problem: _____

4. **Solution:** Run it under cold water.

   Problem: _____

5. **Solution:** Grease the pan first.

   Problem: _____

6. **Solution:** Wash your hair.

   Problem: _____

7. **Solution:** Use a paper towel.

   Problem: _____

8. **Solution:** Throw it out.

   Problem: _____

9. **Solution:** Rub it with alcohol.

   Problem: _____

10. **Solution:** Take two aspirins.

   Problem: _____

11. **Solution:** Put a cast on it.

   Problem: _____

12. **Solution:** Fill it with putty.

   Problem: _____

13. **Solution:** Rake them up.

   Problem: _____

14. **Solution:** Duplicate them.

   Problem: _____

15. **Solution:** Call the police.

   Problem: _____

16. **Solution:** Take it in for a tune-up.

    Problem: _____

17. **Solution:** Return it to the store.

    Problem: _____

18. **Solution:** Use your windshield wipers.

    Problem: _____

19. **Solution:** Wear a pair of boots.

    Problem: _____

20. **Solution:** Look it up in the Yellow Pages.

    Problem: _____

21. **Solution:** Put it back in the oven.

    Problem: _____

22. **Solution:** Turn on the lights.

   Problem: _____

23. **Solution:** Put on a sweater.

   Problem: _____

24. **Solution:** Write a check.

   Problem: _____

25. **Solution:** Sew it on.

   Problem: _____

26. **Solution:** Put it in the dryer.

   Problem: _____

27. **Solution:** Iron it.

   Problem: _____

Target Area 2 Problem Solving | Deciding Factors in Making Decisions

DIRECTIONS: Answer each of the questions on the lines provided.

EXAMPLE: What are two things you would want to know before you register for a night class?

1. *what day it meets on*
2. *how much it costs*

1. What are two things you would want to know before you would buy a house?

    1. _____

    2. _____

2. What are two things you would want to know before you would rent a piano?

    1. _____

    2. _____

3. What are two things you would want to know before you would adopt a child?

    1. _____

    2. _____

4. What are two things you would want to know before you would join a religious group?

   1. _____

   2. _____

5. What are two things you would want to know before you would attend a concert?

   1. _____

   2. _____

6. What are two things you would want to know before you would buy a used car?

   1. _____

   2. _____

7. What are two things you would want to know before you would buy a plane ticket?

   1. _____

   2. _____

8. What are two things you would want to know before you would lend money to someone?

   1. _____

   2. _____

9. What are two things you would want to know before you would sell some antiques?

   1. _____

   2. _____

10. What are two things you would want to know before you would invest in stock?

    1. _____

    2. _____

11. What are two things you would want to know before you would accept a job offer?

    1. _____

    2. _____

12. What are two things you would want to know before you would take a prescribed medication?

    1. _____

    2. _____

13. What are two things you would want to know before you would buy a stereo?

    1. _____

    2. _____

14. What are two things you would want to know before you would open a charge account?

   1. _____

   2. _____

15. What are two things you would want to know before you would check into a motel?

   1. _____

   2. _____

16. What are two things you would want to know before you would hire a lawyer?

   1. _____

   2. _____

17. What are two things you would want to know about a person before you would marry that person?

   1. _____

   2. _____

18. What are two things you would want to know before you would join an exercise club?

   1. _____

   2. _____

19. What are two things you would want to know before you would sign a lease?

    1. _____

    2. _____

20. What are two things you would want to know before you would open a savings account at a bank?

    1. _____

    2. _____

21. What are two things you would want to know before you have some surgery?

    1. _____

    2. _____

22. What are two things you would want to know before you would visit a foreign country?

    1. _____

    2. _____

Target Area 2
Problem Solving | Determining Pros and Cons

DIRECTIONS: Each item describes some situation a person might be in. Think of one advantage and one disadvantage of each situation and write them on the lines.

EXAMPLE: making your own clothes

    Advantage: *it saves money*

    Disadvantage: *it takes a lot of time*

1. being a movie star

    Advantage: _____

    Disadvantage: _____

2. living in an apartment

    Advantage: _____

    Disadvantage: _____

3. having a dog or cat

    Advantage: _____

    Disadvantage: _____

4. having a brother or sister

   Advantage: _____

   Disadvantage: _____

5. living in a city

   Advantage: _____

   Disadvantage: _____

6. being a doctor

   Advantage: _____

   Disadvantage: _____

7. being a child

   Advantage: _____

   Disadvantage: _____

8. owning your own business

   Advantage: _____

   Disadvantage: _____

9. living alone

   Advantage: _____

   Disadvantage: _____

137

10. growing your own vegetables

   Advantage: _____

   Disadvantage: _____

11. being wealthy

   Advantage: _____

   Disadvantage: _____

12. living in a warm climate year round

   Advantage: _____

   Disadvantage: _____

13. being a twin

   Advantage: _____

   Disadvantage: _____

14. being the President of the United States or the First Lady

   Advantage: _____

   Disadvantage: _____

15. going to college

   Advantage: _____

   Disadvantage: _____

16. being a chef

   Advantage: _____

   Disadvantage: _____

17. painting your own house

   Advantage: _____

   Disadvantage: _____

18. being on a diet

   Advantage: _____

   Disadvantage: _____

19. being short

   Advantage: _____

   Disadvantage: _____

20. being married

   Advantage: _____

   Disadvantage: _____

21. having a charge card

   Advantage: _____

   Disadvantage: _____

Target Area 2
Problem Solving | Finding Solutions to Multi-Factor Problems

DIRECTIONS: Read each paragraph and answer the question at the end of it. Write an answer to the question on the lines below the paragraph. Use complete sentences.

EXAMPLE: Tom is painting the walls of his living room. He has a wall and a half left to paint but only enough paint to finish about two-thirds of a wall. He will have to buy another gallon to finish the room. The paint had to be specially mixed and was very expensive. What would you do if you were Tom and wanted to save money?

I would paint the other wall a different color.

1. Helen had received 3 annoying phone calls since midnight. Each time, when she picked up the receiver she heard only heavy breathing. She asked who it was, but got no answer. She then told the caller to stop bothering her. It is now 2:00 A.M., and the phone is ringing. If you were Helen, what would you do?

2. Ted was standing in a check-out line in a grocery store. From out of nowhere, a young boy appeared, pushed him out of line, and rolled his cart aside. He then tried to push by Ted. If you were Ted, what would you do?

3. Bob has a lot of leaves in his yard. He wants to get rid of them. He could put the leaves in garbage bags and leave them for the trash collector. He could go to city hall and apply for a permit to burn them. If you were Bob, what would you do and why?

4. It is Monday, and the Jones family learn that their heat, water, and electricity are going to be shut off from Thursday to Sunday afternoon because of a county project. The temperatures are predicted to be 40 to 50 degrees all weekend. What would you suggest the Joneses do?

5. Jackie has spent too long sunbathing on the beach on the first day of her vacation. She has a very red and painful sunburn. If you were in Jackie's situation, what would you do right away and what would you do for the next few days?

6. Sharon is in a small jewelry store looking at rings. At another counter about 20 feet to her left, she hears a gasp and someone say, "This is a stick-up." She looks over and sees a man pointing a gun at a clerk. He is not looking at her. If you were Sharon, what would you do?

7. John comes home from high school saying that he wants to drop out because he is sick of it and hates it. He can get a full-time job as a waiter at a local restaurant where he now works after school. John has a year and a half to go before he graduates. If you were John's parents, how would you handle the situation?

8. Jenny does not know how to swim. She and her husband are invited to go canoeing with a group of friends and then out for dinner. She wants to go but is scared the canoe might tip. If you were Jenny, what would you do?

9. Ann answers the door one morning, and 2 people are there with literature and a Bible. They want to come in and talk about their religious beliefs. If you were Ann, what would you do?

10. Ray is an independent truck driver for a large company. There are unionized drivers working for the same company. One morning, these other truckers are picketing outside the loading docks when Ray arrives. They do not want him to cross the picket line. If you were Ray, what would you do?

11. Mr. and Mrs. J. Doe live in a nice subdivision. A house on their block has recently been bought by a state agency to be used as a home for 5 mentally impaired adults and their supervisor. The adults will be working in special jobs during the week and will be living in the group home instead of an institution. Some people in the Does' neighborhood are trying to stop them from moving in. If you were Mr. or Mrs. Doe, how would you feel about it and what would you do?

12. Bill drives to work with Rick and Mike. They all work in the same building but in different offices. They alternate drivers. Whenever Rick drives, he is always 15 or 20 minutes late. This doesn't seem to bother Mike, but Bill is upset by it. He has missed the beginning of some meetings because of it. If you were Bill, what would you do?

13. Janet is invited to have her birthday dinner with the Smiths. She is allergic to some foods. If she eats them, she gets what seems like a cold for several days. The Smiths' meal is almost entirely made up of Janet's forbidden foods. If you were Janet, what would you do?

14. George was at a nice, expensive restaurant and ordered a steak cooked rare. When his meal arrived, his vegetables were cold and his steak was overcooked. If you were George, what would you do?

_____

_____

15. Cindy was babysitting for Jason, a five-year-old child. His parents were at a movie. Jason fell and cut his lip and chipped a tooth. Cindy was able to stop the bleeding, but Jason wouldn't stop crying. If you were Cindy, what would you do?

_____

_____

16. Carol is upstairs in bed reading when she thinks she hears a noise downstairs. Her husband will not be back for two hours, and no one else is home. She hears another noise, which she thinks sounds like a door closing. If you were Carol, what would you do?

_____

_____

17. Steven is in the hardware store looking for 5 items to complete a project. He finds 3 of them. He doesn't see a sales clerk around. If you were Steven and wanted to complete the project today, what would you do?

_____

_____

18. Jean and Ed are married. Ed has a drinking problem, but he will not admit it. Jean wants him to get help, but he won't. Last night he came home more drunk than usual, knocked a lamp over, threw a chair, then made nasty remarks to Jean. He tried to hit her, but missed. If you were in Jean's situation, what would you do that night and what would you do the next day?

Target Area 3
FOLLOWING DIRECTIONS

Target Area 3
Following Directions | Following Instructions by Marking Words

DIRECTIONS: Follow the directions given in each item.

EXAMPLE: Put an **X** on the brightest color.

    gray   tan   ~~yellow~~

---

1. Circle the distance that is the longest.

    yard   mile   foot

---

2. Draw a line under the hardest thing.

    rock   cotton   hamburger

---

3. Put an **X** on the oldest one.

    infant   man   teenager

---

4. Put a ring around the thing that belongs in a bathroom.

    knife   towel   blanket

5. Cross out everything except what a fish could eat.

    peanut   bone   worm

---

6. Cross out the smallest number.

    fifty-six   forty-seven   eighty

---

7. Put quotes around your answer to this question.

    Do you ever wear a watch? _____

---

8. Answer this question wrong.

    Does money grow on trees? _____

---

9. Write the answer to this question twice.

    How many cents are in a dime? _____

---

10. Copy these words in reverse order.

    _____

---

11. Put 2 lines under the odd numbers.

    27   34   92   81   45   9

12. Write the word **creative** backwards.

_____

13. Draw a circle, then put a check to the left of it.

_____

14. Write your phone number on the line below. Circle any threes in it, cross out any sixes, underline any ones and twos.

_____

15. On the right line, make a circle. On the left line, put **435**. Make a plus sign between the middle line and the one with the circle on it.

    _____   _____   _____

_____

16. Look at the five words below. Put a star to the left of the second word from the left. Put 2 dots above the shortest word. Circle the word to the east of **phone.** Put the four-letter word in quotes.

    gate   phone   storm   deliver   pin

Target Area 3
Following Directions | Recognizing Incorrect Answers

DIRECTIONS: Each of these questions has been answered. Some of the answers are wrong. Put an **X** on the line by the word **right** if the answer marked is right. Put an **X** on the line by the word **wrong** if the answer marked is wrong.

EXAMPLE: Circle the food. ___ right __X__ wrong

    red   <u>soup</u>   open

---

1. Draw a line over **grape.** ___ right ___ wrong

    group   gripe   <u>grape</u>

---

2. Check the largest animal. ___ right ___ wrong

    beaver   ✓ lion   rabbit

---

3. Circle the second word. ___ right ___ wrong

    allow   big   (order)

---

4. Put a box around the color. ___ right ___ wrong

    [blue]   watch   paper

5. Put an **X** to the left of **many**. ____ right ____ wrong

    organ   first   many ✗

---

6. Check all the words ending in **s**. ____ right ____ wrong

    ✓ scarf   bus   ✓ saddle   genius

---

7. Circle the words that are not abbreviations. ____ right ____ wrong

    etc   (hat)   mr   lb

---

8. Cross out the things you eat. ____ right ____ wrong

    p̶i̶z̶z̶a̶   beer   pens   s̶a̶l̶a̶d̶

---

9. Check every other number. ____ right ____ wrong

    2 ✓   3 ✓   4 ✓   5 ✓   6 ✓

---

10. Draw a line through the sixth **0**. ____ right ____ wrong

    0   0   0   0   0̶   0   0   0   0

---

11. Draw a line above each state. ____ right ____ wrong

    ‾Alaska   Chicago   Denver   ‾Maine

12. Put a triangle under the animals.   _____ right _____ wrong

    raccoon   crow   rabbit   fish
    △   △

13. Put **14** on the third line.   _____ right _____ wrong

    _____   _14_   _____   _____

14. Put a check to the left of the numbers.   _____ right _____ wrong

    ✓4   ✓6   Q   ✓2   ✓5   B

15. Draw 2 circles on the first line.   _____ right _____ wrong

    __O__   __O__   _____

16. Cross out the even numbers.   _____ right _____ wrong

    ~~34~~   ~~42~~   57   ~~66~~   81

17. Write **2** on the line next to **acorn.**   _____ right _____ wrong

    _____ apron   _2_ acorn   _____ across

18. Underline all the furniture.   _____ right _____ wrong

    basket   (desk)   (sofa)   iron

Target Area 3
Following Directions | Following Unrelated Instructions

DIRECTIONS: Read the directions in each sentence and do as they say.

EXAMPLE: Write the last four letters of the alphabet on the line. _WXYZ_

1. Put a line through this entire sentence.

2. Circle the shortest word in this sentence.

3. If there are twelve in a dozen, circle the last word in this sentence.

4. Write the last letter of this month next to this sentence.

5. Cross out the word that has a capital letter in it.

6. Put a question mark over the period at the end of this sentence.

7. Underline the word in this sentence that has less than three letters.

8. Circle the last word in the last sentence on this page.

9. Draw a line through every **e** and circle every **a** in this sentence.

10. Put today's date in the upper left corner of this page.

11. Put an **X** through sentence number 15 on this page.

12. Draw 2 small circles next to the word DIRECTIONS on the previous page.

13. Draw a line through the fifth word in sentence number 11.

14. Put a box around the word **box.**

15. Put your initials next to the period.

16. Write the numbers 1 through 5 along the bottom of this page.

17. Circle the word **circle** twice.

18. Check each word in this sentence, starting with the fourth word.

19. Print the letter **R** after the last word in number 17.

20. Don't do anything to this sentence.

21. Go back to question 2 and cross out the word **sentence.**

22. Draw an **X** through every word in this sentence that has less than five letters in it.

23. Put dots at the beginning and end of sentence 20.

Target Area 3
Following Directions

Decoding If/Then Statements

DIRECTIONS: Read the directions in each sentence and do as they say.

EXAMPLE: If California is larger than Vermont, circle the larger number.
If Vermont is larger, circle the smaller number.

(56)   27

1. If a quarter is worth less than a dime, write **seven.** If not, write **eleven.** _____

2. If a thistle is worn on your finger when you are sewing, write **finger.** If a thistle is a plant with prickly leaves, write **plant.**

_____

3. If ham is meat from a pig, write **pork.** If it is meat from a cow, write **beef.** _____

4. If the sun is larger than the moon, complete this sentence: there are 24 _____ in a day. If the earth is larger than the sun, write **earth:** _____

5. If scar comes before wound in the alphabet,

   check here: _____. If it does not, check here: _____.

---

6. If March comes before April, write a food you don't like. If

   April comes before March, write a food you do like. _____

---

7. If today is a weekday, write the name of a car. If it isn't, write

   the name of a TV program. _____

---

8. If you like tea better than coffee, don't write anything on the

   line. If you like coffee better than tea, put an **X** on the line. If

   you don't like either one, put a dash on the line. _____

---

9. If you are older than 40, write the present year. If you are not,

   write today's date. _____

---

10. If a cow is smaller than a pig, draw an arrow pointing to the

    right. If it is not, draw an arrow pointing to the left. _____

11. If a necklace is longer than a belt, write the name of a president of the U.S. on the line. If it is not, write your last name.

   _____

12. If ice cream comes in flavors, put a check on the second line. If it also comes in colors, put a cross on the last line.

   _____   _____   _____

13. If you can drink from a mug or a thermos, go on to the next question. If you can't, put the number 15 on the line. _____

14. If Kissinger is a comedian, circle his name. If Berle is a comedian, circle Kissinger.

15. If July has a holiday in it, cross out the word July. If it doesn't, write July on the line. _____

16. If you are left-handed, write **right** on the line. If you are right-handed, write **left.** _____

17. If calendars are used for figuring numbers and calculators are used for figuring dates, write your initials. If it is the other way around, write your initials backwards. _____

18. If you listen to a radio and watch TV, check here. _____

    If it is the other way around, check here. _____

19. If Charlie McCarthy, Kermit the Frog, and E.T. are all puppets, write the number **5** on the line. If two of them are puppets, write **3**. If only 1 of them is a puppet, write **1**. _____

20. If tables have 4, stools have 3, and chairs have 2 legs, skip this question. If that is wrong, cross out the wrong number or numbers and put the correct one next to it.

21. If today's date is an odd number, put an **X** on the third line. If the date is an even number, put a check on the first line.

    _____   _____   _____

22. DIRECTIONS: Read the four statements. If the first one is correct, write **yes** on the line after it. If the second statement is correct, write **cold** on the line after it. If the third statement is correct, write **maybe** after it. If the fourth statement is correct, write **no** after it.

   A. Butter should be kept cold, but not milk. _____

   B. Milk should be kept cold, but not butter. _____

   C. Neither butter nor milk should be kept cold. _____

   D. Both butter and milk should be kept cold. _____

23. DIRECTIONS: Read the four statements. If only the first statement is true, put a circle on the first line. If only two of the four statements are true, put a circle on the third line. If all four statements are true, put a circle on the last line. If the first and second statements are both true, put a **+** on the first line. If the third and fourth statements are both true, put a **−** on the fourth line. If the second and third statements are both true, put **OK** on the second line.

   A. Peas and lettuce are fruits. _____

   B. Peas and lettuce are green. _____

   C. Peas and lettuce are vegetables. _____

   D. Peas and lettuce are fattening. _____

**Target Area 3
Following Directions** | **Positioning Letters from Directions**

DIRECTIONS: Read each set of directions, and put the letters on the lines as instructed.

EXAMPLE: Put an **N** on the third line.

On the line before the **N,** put a **U.**

Put an **S** on the remaining line.

<u>　S　</u>　　<u>　U　</u>　　<u>　N　</u>

---

1. Put an **M** on the first line.

   Put a **T** on the last line.

   Put an **A** next to the **T.**

   ___   ___   ___

---

2. Put these words in alphabetical order, then write the first letter of each word in alphabetical order on the lines, starting at the left.

   fan　　even　　miss　　risk　　tense　　or

   ___   ___   ___   ___   ___   ___

3. Put the first 2 letters of **pattern** on lines 1 and 2.

   Put the last 2 letters of **chart** on lines 3 and 4.

   ___   ___   ___   ___
    1   2   3   4

---

4. In the word **light,** cross out the **L, G,** and **H** and put the remaining letters on lines 1 and 2.

   In the word **bet,** cross out the **B** and **T** and put the remaining letter on line 3.

   In the word **home,** pick one letter to put on line 4 so that all of the letters on the lines form a word.

   ___   ___   ___   ___
    1   2   3   4

---

5. Put an **R** on line 5.

   Put another **R** to the left of the first one.

   Put an **H** on line 2.

   Put a **Y** to the right of the R.

   Put a **C** to the left of the H.

   Put an **E** on the remaining line.

   ___   ___   ___   ___   ___   ___
    1   2   3   4   5   6

6. Put the third letter of **ear** on line 3.

   Put the last letter of **deep** on line 1.

   Put the second letter of **dance** on line 2.

   Put the sixth letter of **intention** on line 4.

   ___   ___   ___   ___
    1   2   3   4

---

7. Put the letter that is in both **under** and **suit** on line 3.

   Put the letter that is in both **regent** and **politics** on line 5.

   Put the letter that is in both **actor** and **child** on line 1.

   Put the letter that is in both **tour** and **accept** on line 4.

   Put the letter that is in both **motion** and **alcohol** on line 2.

   ___   ___   ___   ___   ___
    1   2   3   4   5

Target Area 3
Following Directions

Answering Questions with Figures and Symbols

DIRECTIONS: Look at the figures. Then read the questions and write the answers on the lines.

[R] (P) S

EXAMPLE: Which letter is in a box? __R__

What is circled? __P__

---

1. (7) /J\ [M] :Y:

Which letter is in a triangle? _____

Which letter has dots around it? _____

Which letter is in a box? _____

---

2. **RB   TQ   AB   YT**

Which letter is beside a Q? _____

Which pair of letters is in alphabetical order? _____

Which two are farthest away in the alphabet? _____

3. **62   39   47   13**

Which number is the second largest? _____

Which number is closest to 40? _____

Which number is to the right of 47? _____

---

4. **Q   P   R   S**

Which letter is to the left of the P? _____

Which letter is the farthest to the right? _____

Write the letters in alphabetical order. _____

---

5. **−   +   ÷   ×**

Does the sign next to × mean to divide? _____

Does the sign to the west of ÷ mean to subtract? _____

What is the third sign? _____

6. **9:15   95% $1.65   1¾**

   Which number shows a fraction? _____

   Which has to do with A.M. or P.M.? _____

   Which shows a percentage? _____

---

7. **XO   XX   OX   OO**

   What is to the left of XX? _____

   What is to the right of OX? _____

   What comes before XX? _____

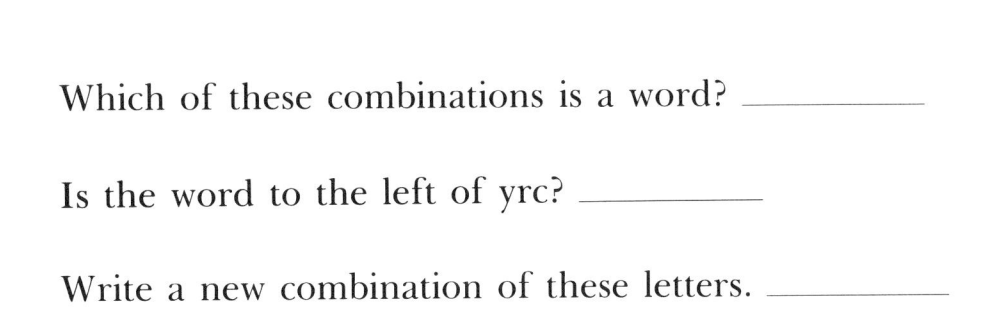

---

8. **cyr   yrc   cry   ycr**

   Which of these combinations is a word? _____

   Is the word to the left of yrc? _____

   Write a new combination of these letters. _____

Target Area 3
Following Directions

Understanding Spatial Relationships

DIRECTIONS: Look at the figures on this page. Then read the questions on the opposite page. Look at these figures to answer the questions.

EXAMPLE: What numbers are in the circle? __8, 9__

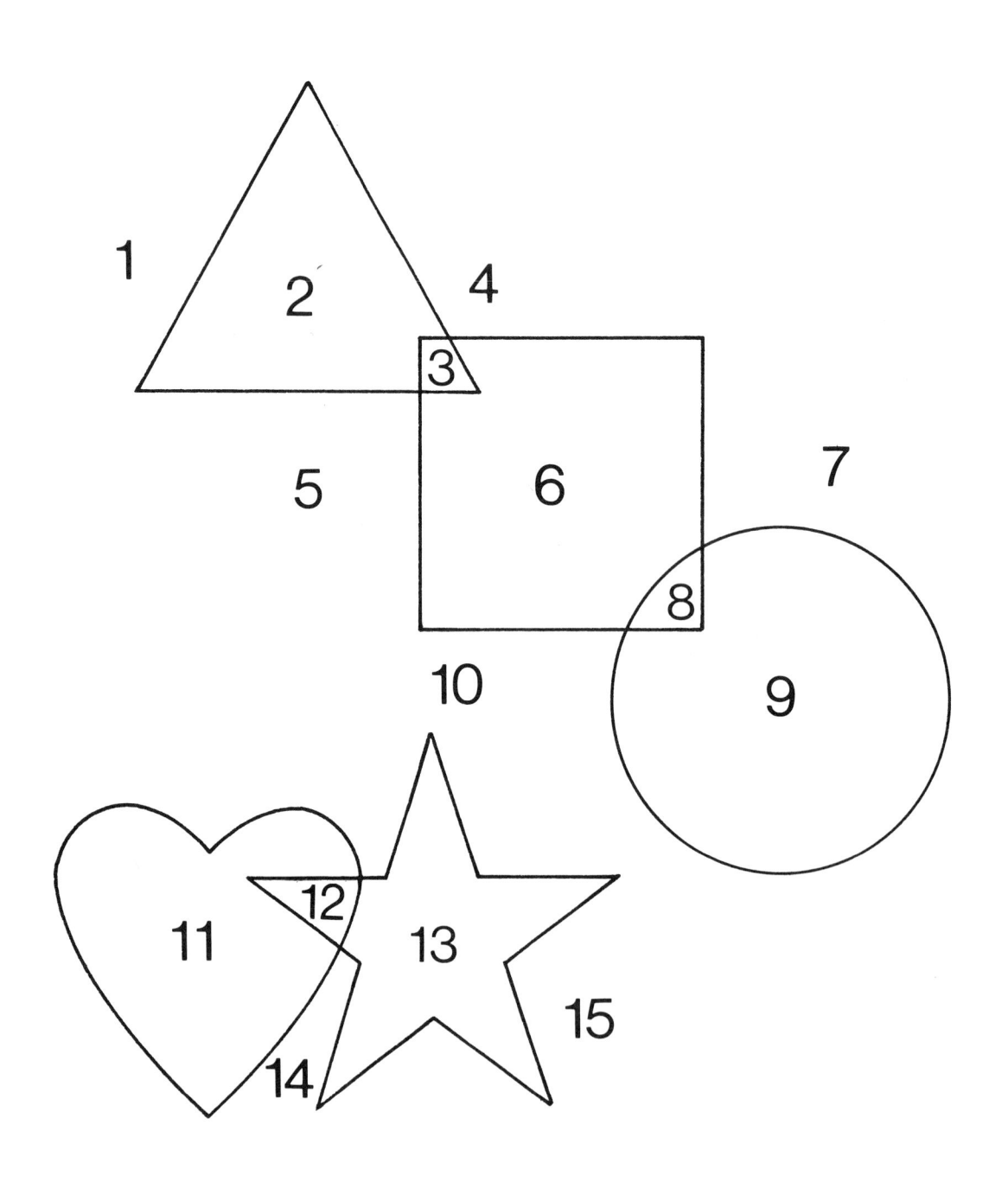

Write the number which is

1. to the right of the square and not in the circle _____

2. in the star and not in the heart _____

3. below the triangle _____

4. in the circle and in the square _____

5. only in the square _____

6. not in the star but in the heart _____

7. in the square and the triangle _____

8. between the star and the heart _____

9. to the left of the triangle _____

10. between the heart and star but not in either one _____

11. above the square and to the right of the triangle _____

12. in the heart and the star _____

13. all the numbers in two figures at once _____

Target Area 3
Following Directions

Understanding Spatial Directions

DIRECTIONS: Follow the directions in each item. Use the boxes for your answers.

EXAMPLE:

In the left box, put **3**.
Darken the box on the right.

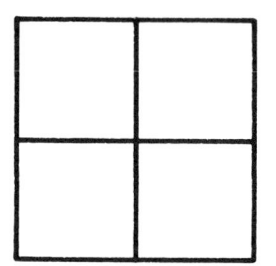

In the upper left box, draw 3 dots.
In the box next to the dots, draw an **A.**
In the lower right box, draw a star.
In the box below the dots, draw a circle.

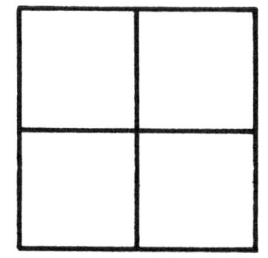

In the box on the lower right, draw a cross.
Blacken the box above the cross.
Next to the blackened box, draw a star.
In the box below the star, write any number.

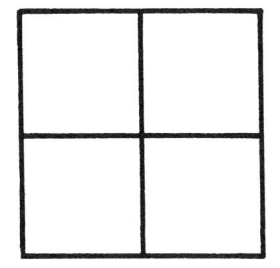

Pick any box and put **2** in it.
In the box in the opposite corner from the one with 2 in it, put **1**.
Next to the box with 1, put **4**.
In the empty box, put **7**.

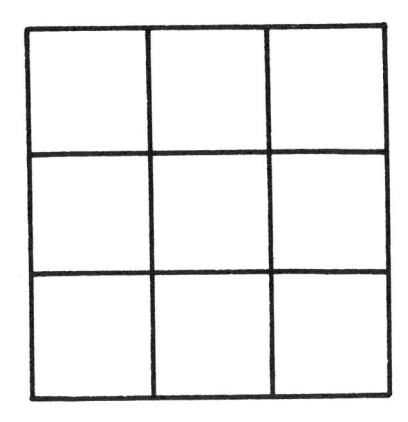

Put an **X** in the third box in the second row.
Put **B** in the box above the one with the **X**.
In the first box in the last row, put an arrow.
Put a circle in the center box.
Put a short vertical line in the box above the arrow.
In one of the remaining corner boxes, put **C**.

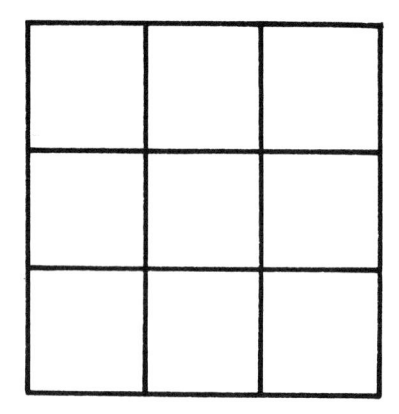

In the middle box, draw a star.
In the box in the upper right corner, put **B.**
Put **1** in the box below the star.
In the second box in the top row, draw a circle.
In the third box of the third row, make a cross from corner to corner.
Put your initials in the empty box in the bottom row.

DIRECTIONS: Answer the questions about the boxes on the lines.

What is below the dots? _____

What is to the right of the square? _____

What is the letter? _____

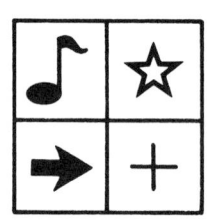

What is in the upper left square? _____

What figure does the arrow point to? _____

What is above the + ? _____

In the row with the letters, write the middle letter. _____

What is the third shape in the top row? _____

What number is below **R**? _____

What is in the top box on the right? _____

What is above **B**? _____

What is above the bottom box in the last row? _____

What is in the middle box in the top row? _____

What is to the left of the shaded box? _____

What is in the box below the dash? _____

Is the box below **A** empty? _____

Target Area 3
Following Directions | Drawing by Instruction

DIRECTIONS: Follow the directions for each question, using the space below the directions.

EXAMPLE: Draw a horizontal line about 2 inches long.
Make an X to the left of the line.

X ———————

---

1. In the space below, draw 2 large circles next to each other.
   Draw a line under both circles.
   Draw a dot in the center of the circle on the left.
   Draw a small triangle in the circle on the right.
   Write any number in the space between the circles.

2. Make 4 dots in the center of the box below.
   Write the numbers from 1 to 5 down the left side of the box.
   Draw a small triangle in the bottom right corner of the box.
   Between the dots and the top of the box, write today's date.
   Draw a line from number 4 to the triangle.
   Draw a rectangle in the bottom half of the box.
   Inside the rectangle draw a circle.

3. Draw a long horizontal line in the middle of the space below.
   Draw a vertical line through the horizontal line to divide it in half.
   To the right of the vertical line and below the horizontal line, make a small oval.
   To the left of the vertical line and above the horizontal line, make 2 small wavy lines.
   Above the oval, put 2 numbers between 1 and 50.

4. Write any 2 letters in the right half of the circle.
   Put the number 7 near the top of the circle.
   Draw an arrow that points from the letters to the number.
   Draw a small heart in the center of the circle.
   Make a line from the heart to the bottom of the circle.
   Put an X somewhere on the line.

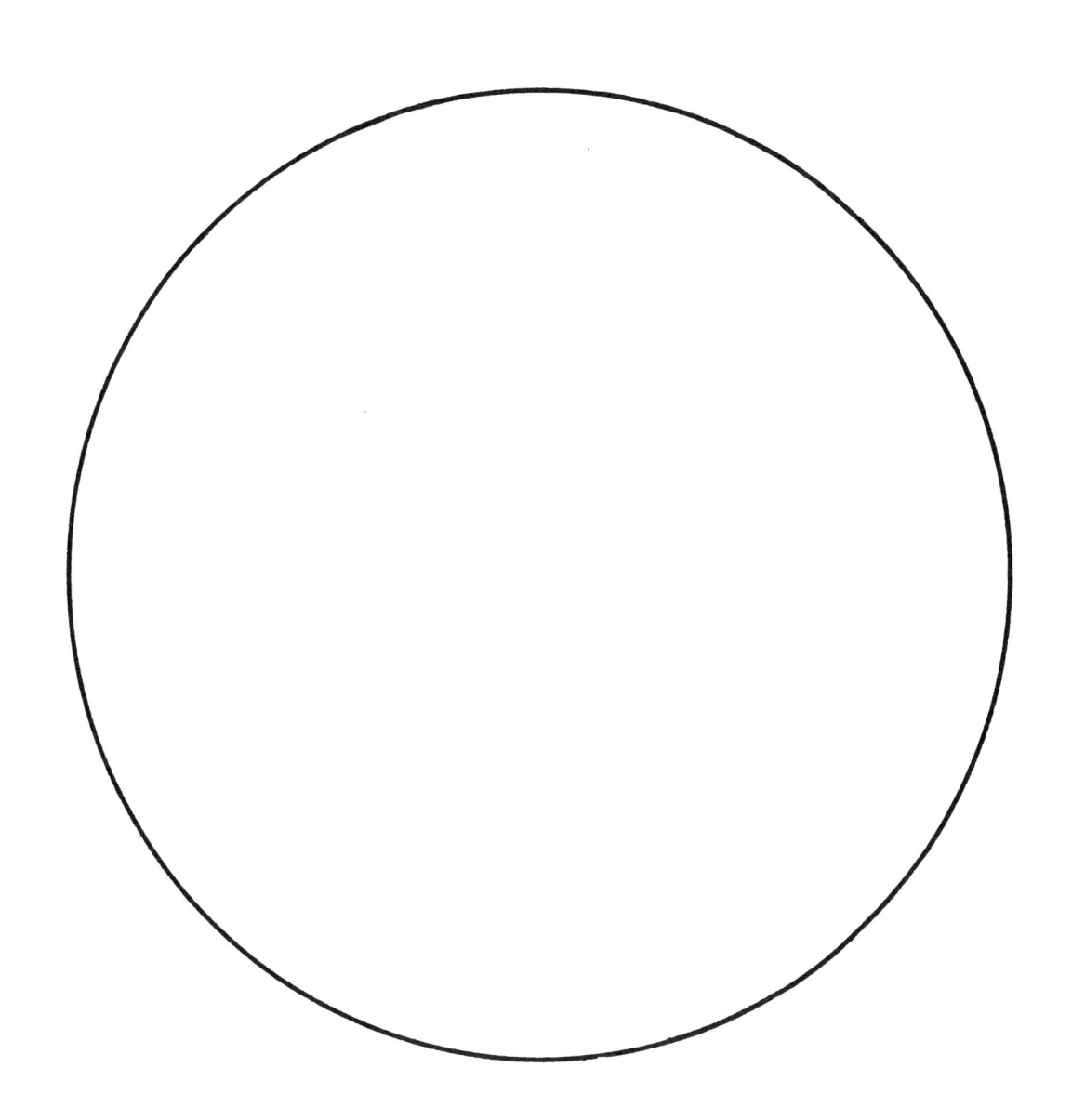

5. Draw a small circle in the square.
   In the first figure, put 4 small dots.
   Draw a wavy line between the dots and the circle.
   Connect the second and third figures with a line.
   Put 4 short lines in the triangle.
   Put an X in the top part of the cross.

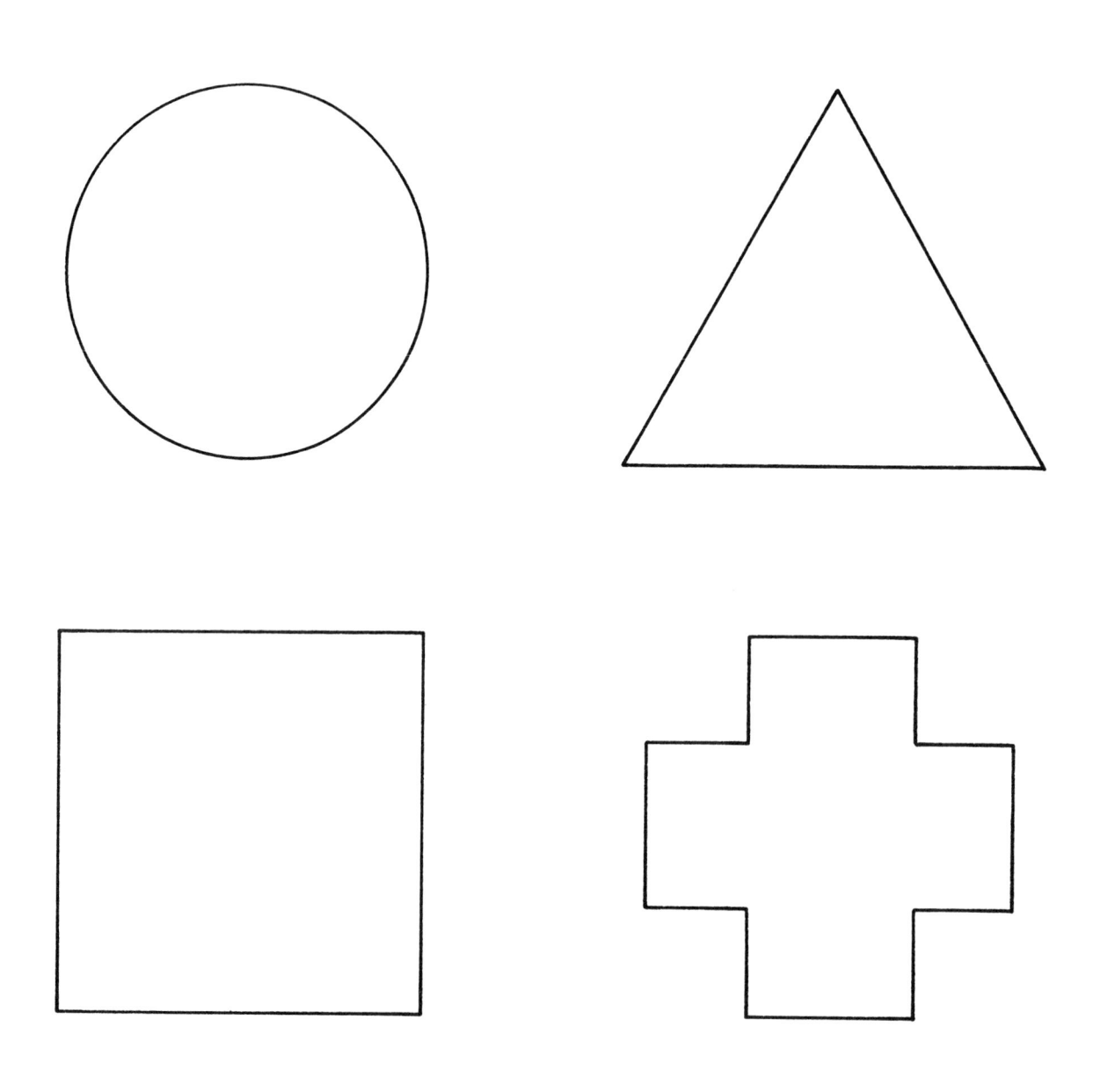

Target Area 3
Following Directions | Locating Information

DIRECTIONS: Read the directions. Write the answer on the line.

EXAMPLE: Turn to the next page. Write the first word on that page on the line. *Look*

1. Turn to page 81, and write the first word on that page. _____

2. Turn to page 47, and write the answer to question 16. _____

3. Look in a telephone book, and write the name of the first person listed. _____

4. Look up September 14 on a calendar, and write the day of the week that it falls on this year. _____

5. Look on a telephone dial, and write the letters you see next to number 6. _____

177

6. Look up Z in a dictionary, and write the last two words listed. _____

7. Look on the title page of a book, and write the name of the publisher and the copyright date. _____

8. Turn to the Contents in this book, and write the page number of the third exercise in Target Area 4. _____

9. Look at a newspaper, and copy 2 headlines from the front page. _____

10. Copy the serial number of an appliance on the right line, and write the name of the appliance on the left line. _____

11. Look in a TV guide, and write the names of 2 programs that you could watch at 7:30 P.M. Thursday evening. _____

12. Write the return address from a letter you received.

_____

_____

13. Look at a jar of something (like mustard or salad dressing), and write the ingredients in it. _____

_____

14. Turn to the back of this book, and write the last page number that you see. _____

15. Turn to page 198 and write the answer to the example that is given there. _____

Target Area 3
Following Directions | Filling Out Forms

DIRECTIONS: This page looks like some kind of application form. Read the instructions below each line carefully. Then fill out the information asked for.

EXAMPLE:

INSURANCE STATUS: ☐ ☒ ☐

      If you are a member of Blue Cross, put an X in the second box.
      If you are a member of some other medical plan, put an X in the third box.

NAME: _____
      Print your last name here.

NAME: _____
      Write your first name, a comma, then your middle initial.

ADDRESS: _____
      Write your address, street name first, number next.

PHONE: _____
      Write your phone number with area code in parentheses.

CITIZENSHIP: _____
      If you are a citizen of a country other than the U.S., write the name of that country on the line.

MARITAL STATUS: ☐ ☐ ☐

      If single, check the second box.
      If married, darken the last box.
      If in school, cross out the first box.

TYPE OF DWELLING: _____

        Use these abbreviations: apartment-ment, house-use, condominium-dom, own-O, rent-R

SIBLINGS: _____

        If you are an only child, write yes. If not, write first the number of sisters you have, then the number of brothers.

EMPLOYMENT: _____

        If presently employed, write the name of your employer. If not employed, cross out the word employment.

SOCIAL SECURITY: _____ _____ _____

        Write the first 3 numbers on the second line, and the rest of the numbers on the third line.

STATUS: _____

        Do not write on this line.

BIRTHDAY: _____

        Use entire words, no abbreviations.

BANK: _____

        Name of your bank and city it is in.

AUTO: _____

        Color of your car, make, and year of purchase.

EDUCATION: _____

        Print the name of the school you last attended.

MEDICAL HISTORY: Put a check next to those conditions you have experienced. Put a circle on the line if you have had the condition more than once.

_____ allergies

_____ appendicitis

_____ broken leg

_____ broken arm

_____ diarrhea

_____ earache

_____ pneumonia

_____ sore throat

_____ stiff neck

_____ stroke

_____ surgery

_____ tonsillectomy

If you checked any of the above, write the approximate date on which it occurred in the space below.

Target Area 4
VISUAL/LOGICAL SEQUENCING

Target Area 4
Visual/Logical Sequencing | Separating Words

DIRECTIONS: Draw a vertical line between the different words as the directions indicate.

EXAMPLE: Draw lines between the numbers.

SIX|NINE|TWO|SEVEN|ONE

---

1. Draw lines between the colors.

    REDBLUEBLACKORANGEYELLOW

---

2. Draw lines between the musical instruments.

    VIOLINGUITARDRUMSFLUTEPIANOTRUMPETTUBA

---

3. Draw lines between the fruits.

    BANANAAPPLEPEARGRAPEPLUMLIME

---

4. Draw lines between the cities.

    PHOENIXATLANTASEATTLECHICAGOORLANDO

5. Draw lines between the pieces of furniture.

CHAIRCOUCHLAMPCHESTBOOKCASELOVESEAT

6. Draw lines between the months.

DECEMBEROCTOBERMAYAUGUSTMARCHAPRIL

7. Draw lines between the tools.

RAKEHAMMERSHOVELSCREWDRIVERPLIERSHOE

8. Draw lines between the parts of the body.

LUNGSHIPELBOWANKLESHOULDERHEART

9. Draw lines between the items of clothing.

SHOESBLOUSESHIRTPANTSBELTTIE

10. Draw lines between the flowers.

PANSYROSEDAISYVIOLETSNAPDRAGONLILY

11. Draw lines between the vegetables.

PEASCELERYEGGPLANTCUCUMBERBEANSONION

12. Draw lines between the sports.

GOLFSKIINGTENNISBASEBALLSOCCERHOCKEY

13. Draw lines between the animals.

BEAROPPOSUMGIRAFFELIONWEASELLEOPARD

14. Draw lines between the trees.

MAPLEELMSPRUCEPINECHESTNUTBIRCH

15. Draw lines between the numbers.

TWELVESIXTYNINETYELEVENFIVEONE

16. Draw lines between the states.

COLORADOMAINEKANSASOHIOVIRGINIAUTAH

17. Draw lines between the cars.

CHRYSLERFORDTOYOTABUICKMERCURYPONTIAC

Target Area 4
Visual/Logical Sequencing

Tracking Words

DIRECTIONS: Each line has a 4- or 5-letter word hidden in it. Look for the word, and when you have found it, circle it.

EXAMPLE: e p a s o r e y b r

1. s a b o u t j o n r
2. l o s t i g a h v e
3. e x c a l a r m i n
4. b i b u s o r g a n
5. w e g l o t r i p y
6. s b o l t h n e f t
7. k l e d e v i l i n
8. p l o q u y a r d y
9. d i l i l y o k l y
10. t e j y a t r u e u y

11. q u a p a r t y e r
12. f e l i o b s o c k
13. s r o t i t l e y s
14. t o r o u n d o u n
15. s i b o l o n l y y
16. a i s l e s l a i s
17. m a p o i n t e n z
18. v w i n k u y o n p
19. w e l b o w d e r s
20. f r a g r a b e r s

21. amekachose

22. staigloore

23. terswangey

24. aspringleb

25. joverseoxs

26. brebrosort

27. crangeolre

28. jablegerje

29. shoxpuncho

30. elforcebra

31. fashalfahe

32. dasincelds

33. eagboreder

34. blucroakis

35. grerangled

36. ehighoofle

37. monispalmy

38. tesscarcho

Target Area 4
Visual/Logical Sequencing | Respacing Words

DIRECTIONS: Rewrite each sentence, using the correct spacing between the words. **HINT:** Draw a line between the words before you rewrite them.

EXAMPLE: Turn|o n|th e|li ght.

Turn on the light.

1. Th eflow ersa reon thet able.

2. Pic kup theb ook.

3. Wat erth eplan tbef or eyo ugo.

4. Win teris jus taroun dthecor ner.

5. That gre ens uitiso nsal eun tilth eeleventh.

6. Iw anta ho tfud gesun daewit hnuts.

190

7. Waxth eflo orbe for eyo udust.

8. Juneist hesixt hmo nthoft hey ear.

9. Let tucet oma toesan don ionsare inmys al ad.

10. Six tee nplu sone equa lsse vent een.

11. Itwasa dayfu llofs urp rises.

12. Ane wjew elrys tore haso pen edin them all.

13. Sever alcas esofth efluw erere port ed.

14. Hew assot ire dhef ellas leep righ taw ay.

15. Inas hort time wew ill beh ome.

___

16. Plan ttul ipbul bsint hefa llbe foreaf rost.

___

17. Ra inise xpec tedla terth iswee kend.

___

18. Iw oul dli kes ome cak ean dac upo ftea.

___

19. Rep ort erscr owd edar oundth emov ies tar.

___

20. Brid gesar est ruct ures buil tov erw ate r.

___

Target Area 4
Visual/Logical Sequencing

Answering Alphabet Questions

DIRECTIONS: Write the alphabet, then read each question. Answer it by writing a letter on the line.

EXAMPLE: What letter comes after **P**? *Q*

Write the alphabet here. _____

_____

1. What letter comes before **Q**? _____

2. What letter comes after **U**? _____

3. What letter is 2 letters after **J**? _____

4. What letter is between **C** and **E**? _____

5. What is your middle initial? _____

6. What are the last 4 letters of the alphabet? _____

7. What letter do you usually add to make a word mean more than one thing? _____

8. What is the 6th letter of the alphabet? _____

9. What letter is between **G** and **L** and is a word all by itself? _____

10. What is the next to last letter of the alphabet? _____

11. What letter always follows **Q** in a word? _____

12. What letters are vowels? _____

13. What letter sounds like **ewe**? _____

14. What letter comes between **M** and **O**? _____

15. What letter can sound like an **S** in a word but is another letter? _____

Target Area 4
Visual/Logical Sequencing | Locating Embedded Words

DIRECTIONS: Each of these words has a smaller one within it. Write the smaller word on the line. **HINT**: The letters of the words are in order.

EXAMPLE: charmer *harm*

1. shower _____
2. opening _____
3. factory _____
4. octopus _____
5. rations _____
6. honest _____
7. vanish _____
8. barrier _____
9. thunder _____
10. smuggle _____
11. obedient _____
12. volcano _____
13. branch _____
14. preacher _____
15. apartment _____
16. command _____
17. elevator _____
18. romance _____

DIRECTIONS: Each of these words has two smaller ones within it. Write the two words on the line. **HINT:** The letters of the words are in order.

19. seasonal _____

20. intelligent _____

21. carpenter _____

22. forward _____

23. bandage _____

24. sapphire _____

25. illiterate _____

26. cardinal _____

27. bonnet _____

28. caravan _____

29. martini _____

30. legality _____

31. teasing _____

32. fortunate _____

33. cooperation _____

34. pledging _____

35. atmosphere _____

36. retirement _____

37. capable _____

38. coincidence _____

39. blasting _____

40. restrain _____

Target Area 4
Visual/Logical Sequencing | Rearranging Words

DIRECTIONS: Rearrange the letters in each word so that they form another word. Write the new word on the line.

EXAMPLE: meat *team*

1. eat _____
2. rat _____
3. end _____
4. ram _____
5. ape _____
6. tow _____
7. now _____
8. who _____
9. era _____
10. top _____

11. bore _____
12. pier _____
13. dear _____
14. mane _____
15. lead _____
16. felt _____
17. laid _____
18. lime _____
19. spot _____
20. race _____

21. pale _____

22. cork _____

23. stun _____

24. gulp _____

25. earn _____

26. lame _____

27. loot _____

28. rear _____

29. each _____

30. odor _____

31. keep _____

32. seal _____

33. stud _____

34. state _____

35. charm _____

36. neon _____

37. crate _____

38. devil _____

Target Area 4
Visual/Logical Sequencing | Ranking by Size

DIRECTIONS: There are 5 things named in each item. Number them in order from smallest (**1**) to largest (**5**).

EXAMPLE: roll of Scotch tape *1*
              maple tree *3*
              tape recorder *2*

1. elephant ____
   Mickey Rooney ____
   Eiffel Tower ____
   ladybug ____
   hamster ____

2. Corvette ____
   army tank ____
   roller skate ____
   van ____
   bicycle ____

3. grape ____
   grapefruit ____
   orange ____
   lime ____
   watermelon ____

4. sponge ____
   hair dryer ____
   rubber band ____
   desk ____
   shovel ____

5. fireplace   _____

   truck   _____

   teapot   _____

   needle   _____

   bandage   _____

6. turkey   _____

   apple   _____

   egg   _____

   carton of milk   _____

   vitamin pill   _____

7. toothpick   _____

   toaster oven   _____

   tractor   _____

   box of cereal   _____

   screwdriver   _____

8. paper bag   _____

   piece of paper   _____

   cardboard carton _____

   stamp   _____

   crate   _____

9. telephone book   _____

   Life Magazine   _____

   TV Guide   _____

   file card   _____

   box of matches   _____

10. sheet   _____

    quilt   _____

    pillowcase   _____

    drapes   _____

    hankerchief   _____

11. bowling ball   _____

    marble   _____

    tennis ball   _____

    beach ball   _____

    ping-pong ball   _____

13. bottle of wine   _____

    bottle of ketchup   _____

    jar of mustard   _____

    stick of butter   _____

    can of beer   _____

12. briefcase   _____

    cupcake   _____

    suitcase   _____

    lipstick   _____

    pocketbook   _____

14. cat   _____

    tiger   _____

    giraffe   _____

    squirrel   _____

    fox   _____

Target Area 4
Visual/Logical Sequencing

Ranking by Attributes

DIRECTIONS: Read the directions for each item. Write the words in the order given in the directions.

EXAMPLE: List these in order from smallest to largest.

ocean _____ *stream*

stream _____ *river*

river _____ *lake*

lake _____ *ocean*

---

1. List these in order from hottest to coldest.

    summer _____

    fire _____

    ice cube _____

    room temperature _____

---

2. List these in order from lightest to heaviest.

    one dozen roses _____

    pair of socks _____

    typewriter _____

    rocking chair _____

203

3. List these in order from darkest to brightest.

   sun _____

   sunset _____

   fog _____

   black _____

4. List these from the beginning of the year to the end.

   Halloween _____

   Christmas _____

   Labor Day _____

   Valentine's Day _____

5. List these in order from lowest to highest.

   stool _____

   ladder _____

   chair _____

   highchair _____

6. List these in order from slowest to fastest.

   bicycle _____

   merry-go-round _____

   airplane _____

   train _____

7. List these in order from least tiring to most tiring.

   climbing stairs _____

   walking _____

   sleeping _____

   playing tennis _____

8. List these in order from softest to hardest.

   rock _____

   marshmallow _____

   mattress _____

   modeling clay _____

9. List these in order from quietest to noisiest.

   ticking clock _____

   buzz saw _____

   crickets _____

   silence _____

---

10. List these in order from youngest to oldest.

    senior citizen _____

    adolescent _____

    adult _____

    infant _____

---

11. List these in order from least to most fattening.

    orange _____

    ice cream sundae _____

    hamburger _____

    water _____

12. List these in order from smallest to largest.

   dime _____

   quarter _____

   penny _____

   half-dollar _____

13. List these in order from earliest to latest.

   evening _____

   morning _____

   afternoon _____

   midnight _____

14. List these in order from lightest to heaviest.

   pint _____

   gallon _____

   quart _____

   cup _____

15. List these in order from shortest to longest.

   mile   _____

   foot   _____

   inch   _____

   yard   _____

16. List these in order from shortest to longest.

   decade   _____

   day   _____

   month   _____

   century   _____

Target Area 4
Visual/Logical Sequencing

Sequencing Steps in a Task

DIRECTIONS: Some steps involved in doing something are listed in each item. The steps are mixed up. Number the steps in order from **1** (what to do first) to **4** (what to do last).

EXAMPLE: making soup

    _4_ Heat it.
    _1_ Choose a kind of soup.
    _3_ Put it in a pan.
    _2_ Open the can.

---

1. changing a lightbulb

    ____ Put in the new bulb.
    ____ Remove the old bulb.
    ____ Turn on the light.
    ____ Turn off the light.

---

2. making a cup of tea

    ____ Put the teabag in the cup.
    ____ Boil the water.
    ____ Remove the bag when the tea is ready.
    ____ Put water in the cup.

3. putting up a picture

   _____ Hammer the nail in the wall.
   _____ Mark a spot for the nail.
   _____ Decide where you want the picture.
   _____ Hook the picture wire on the nail.

4. taking out the garbage

   _____ Fasten the bag.
   _____ Go outside.
   _____ Empty the wastebaskets into one large bag.
   _____ Put the bag where it will be picked up.

5. taking a bath

   _____ Get in the tub.
   _____ Turn on the water.
   _____ Check the water temperature.
   _____ Put in the plug.

6. buying candy from a machine

   _____ Take the candy from the slot.
   _____ Get out the correct change.
   _____ Insert the money.
   _____ Pull the lever for your choice.

7. buying a new car

   _____ Talk over the price.
   _____ Decide what make you want.
   _____ Choose the options you want.
   _____ Go to a car dealer.

8. withdrawing money from a bank account

   _____ Fill out a withdrawal slip.
   _____ Enter the numbers in your bankbook.
   _____ Decide the amount of money you need.
   _____ Go to a teller.

9. fixing a cut

   _____ Dry it.
   _____ Clean it.
   _____ Bandage it.
   _____ Put antiseptic on it.

10. going bowling

    _____ Put on bowling shoes.
    _____ Pick up a ball.
    _____ Choose an alley.
    _____ Roll the ball down the alley.

11. getting ready to go out

　　_____ Take a shower.

　　_____ Fix your hair.

　　_____ Put on makeup or shave.

　　_____ Get dressed.

12. taking a plane trip

　　_____ Arrive at the airport.

　　_____ Pay for the ticket.

　　_____ Decide when you want to go.

　　_____ Make a reservation.

13. going to a movie

　　_____ Buy a ticket.

　　_____ Choose the movie you want.

　　_____ Go to the theater.

　　_____ Go inside and sit down.

14. playing cards

　　_____ Deal the cards.

　　_____ Shuffle the cards.

　　_____ Get out the cards.

　　_____ Cut the deck.

Target Area 4
Visual/Logical Sequencing

Sequencing
Informational Statements

DIRECTIONS: A short story is told in each item. Number the statements following each story from **1** to **3** to show what happened first, second, and third in the story.

EXAMPLE: When I finished cooking the rice, I made the salad. Then I checked the roast, which had been cooking for three hours.

1 I made the roast.
3 I made the salad.
2 I made the rice.

---

1. He put on a blue shirt after he took off the pin-striped one. He decided to wear it and also chose a maroon tie.

   _____ He put on a pin-striped shirt.

   _____ He put on a maroon tie.

   _____ He put on a blue shirt.

---

2. They picked 3 quarts of strawberries before noon. They washed and hulled them, then cut them up for strawberry shortcake.

   _____ They made shortcake.

   _____ They hulled the berries.

   _____ They cut up the berries.

3. My dog always chases squirrels after he eats. He always drinks water before he eats, but never afterward.

   _____ The dog eats.

   _____ The dog drinks water.

   _____ The dog chases squirrels.

---

4. Usually I have orange juice for breakfast, but today I had apple juice. Then I made myself toast after I had cereal.

   _____ I had apple juice.

   _____ I had toast.

   _____ I had cereal.

---

5. They went to Chicago on their way to St. Louis. They saw Cincinnati on their way back before they returned to Toledo.

   _____ They went to Cincinnati.

   _____ They went to Chicago.

   _____ They went to St. Louis.

6. They had pizza before the game, popcorn during the game, and hamburgers afterward.

   _____ They ate hamburgers.

   _____ They ate popcorn.

   _____ They ate pizza.

7. Harry sat down next to Bill after he bought popcorn. George arrived first, and saved seats for all of them.

   _____ Harry sat down.

   _____ George sat down.

   _____ Bill sat down.

8. Preheat the oven to 350°. Melt the butter and sugar in a saucepan. While it is cooking, beat two eggs. Add them to the cooled mixture and stir.

   _____ Preheat the oven.

   _____ Mix the eggs, butter, and sugar.

   _____ Melt the sugar and butter.

9. Mrs. Smith has been a widow for 4 years. Her daughter moved out 6 years ago. After her husband died, she bought a dog.

   _____ Her husband died.

   _____ Her daughter moved.

   _____ She bought a dog.

---

10. Joan's birthday is 5 days before Linda's. Sue's birthday is 3 days after Joan's.

    _____ Joan's birthday.

    _____ Linda's birthday.

    _____ Sue's birthday.

---

11. The office building was built in 1977. A wing was added 5 years later. In 1980, the building was repainted.

    _____ The building was repainted.

    _____ The building was built.

    _____ A wing was built.

12. Tom Shaff goes to France in August. He goes to London in April. In November, he goes to Italy.

    _____ He goes to Italy.

    _____ He goes to London.

    _____ He goes to France.

---

13. Today the garbage has to be taken out. Tomorrow the plumber is coming. The day after tomorrow, the car should be washed.

    _____ Take out the garbage.

    _____ Wait for the plumber.

    _____ Wash the car.

---

14. Before the guests arrived, he had started the grill. The appetizers were in the oven.

    _____ The guests arrived.

    _____ He started the grill.

    _____ The appetizers were ready.

15. He picked up the prints at the drugstore. He found 2 he liked and sent them to be enlarged.

 _____ He had the photos developed.

 _____ He had the photos enlarged.

 _____ He took the photographs.

Target Area 5
HUMOR

Target Area 5
Humor
Matching Riddles to Answers

DIRECTIONS: There are 4 riddles and 4 answers in each group. Choose the word which correctly answers each riddle. Write the letter of the correct word on the line next to the riddle.

EXAMPLE: A. fir   B. rainbow

What kind of bow is impossible to tie? __B__

What tree is like a coat? __A__

A. screwdriver   B. bed   C. Mississippi   D. trumpet

What kind of driver doesn't get a speeding ticket? _____

What has 4 eyes? _____

What has 4 legs, but only 1 foot? _____

What pet makes the best music? _____

A. sidewalk   B. slippers   C. mushroom   D. mitten

What shoes can you make from banana peels? _____

What comes to the door but not into the house? _____

What has a thumb but no fingers? _____

What room is never part of a house? _____

A. catfish   B. saw   C. sponge   D. barber

What has lots of teeth but no mouth? _____

What is full of holes yet holds water? _____

What kind of cat isn't afraid of water? _____

Who shaves more than 3 times a day? _____

A. cannibal   B. flypaper   C. envelope   D. window

What material makes the best kite? _____

What gets fed up with people? _____

What lets you see through walls? _____

What word usually contains one letter? _____

A. Ohio   B. wrong   C. hole   D. bulldozer

What is a sleeping bull called? _____

What is round at both ends and high in the middle? _____

What weighs the same no matter how big is is? _____

What word do we always pronounce wrong? _____

A. smoke	B. lap	C. umbrella	D. Pennsylvania

What do you lose when you stand up? _____

What can fill a house but doesn't weigh anything? _____

Where do pencils come from? _____

What goes up when the rain comes down? _____

A. horse	B. comb	C. nightmare	D. watchdog

What has teeth but never eats? _____

What horse stays up the latest? _____

What always goes to bed with shoes on? _____

What animal keeps the best time? _____

A. potato	B. seven	C. mosquito	D. tulips

What flowers do all people have? _____

What insect goes skin diving? _____

What odd number becomes even when you remove the first letter? _____

What has eyes but cannot see? _____

**Target Area 5　　Solving
Humor　　　　　Riddles**

DIRECTIONS:　Each riddle has a choice of 3 answers. Choose the answer which solves the riddle, and circle it.

EXAMPLE:　　What animal keeps the best time?

　　　　lion　　　　　　(watchdog)　　　　　　hen

---

1. What goes out every day but never leaves his home?

　　fly　　　　　　　squirrel　　　　　　　turtle

---

2. What part of a fish weighs the most?

　　scales　　　　　　gills　　　　　　　tail

---

3. What kind of fish would be found in a bird cage?

　　perch　　　　　　canary　　　　　　tuna

---

4. What has a head and tail but no body?

　　dog　　　　　　　penny　　　　　　kite

5. What falls often but never gets hurt?

    bird   snow   boy

---

6. What do frogs sit on at mealtime?

    toadstools   lilypads   chairs

---

7. What kind of key will not open a door?

    master key   skeleton key   monkey

---

8. What bird can you find in your throat?

    robin   swallow   cardinal

---

9. What never asks any questions, but everyone answers it?

    radio   telephone   TV

---

10. What do you call a person who loves hot chocolate?

    coconut   Hershey bar   brownie

11. What kind of coat is always put on wet?

    coat of arms   coat of paint   housecoat

---

12. What kind of nut would you use to hang a picture?

    peanut   almond   walnut

---

13. What belongs to you but others use it more than you do?

    your brush   your name   your clothes

---

14. What kind of stone is a fake?

    shamrock   diamond   pebble

---

15. What is the life story of a car called?

    bibliography   autobiography   assembly line

---

16. What has a hand but no fingers?

    baby   football   clock

17. What do you get when you cross an insect with a rabbit?

    Bumble Bee   Bugs Bunny   Donald Duck

---

18. What 10-letter word starts with GAS?

    typewriter   automobile   gaslight

---

19. What animal doesn't play fairly?

    skunk   pig   cheetah

---

20. What can speak any language in the world?

    linguist   echo   mirror

---

21. Who can stay single even if he marries a lot of people?

    minister   singer   mailman

---

22. What does a cat have that no other animal has?

    paws   fur   kittens

Target Area 5 Humor | Choosing Humorous Answers

DIRECTIONS: Each question has 3 answers. All the answers may fit the sentence, but only one of them is funny. Mark the **funny** answer.

EXAMPLE: Why did the lobster blush?

_____ It was very hot.

__X__ It saw the salad dressing.

_____ It was embarrassed.

---

1. Why do birds fly south?

   _____ To get away from the cold weather.

   _____ It's an instinct; they always do it.

   _____ It's too far to walk.

---

2. Why did the 2 doctors work together?

   _____ They wanted to try a new type of surgery.

   _____ They liked to co-operate.

   _____ They liked to save time.

3. Why is a baseball team like a good pancake?

　　_____　Its success depends on the batter.

　　_____　They both run a lot.

　　_____　They both are good players.

---

4. What is a target range used for?

　　_____　To shoot targets.

　　_____　To cook targets.

　　_____　To practice using a gun.

---

5. What's the difference between a sailor and a shopper?

　　_____　One is on the land; the other is on the water.

　　_____　One sails the sea; the other sees the sale.

　　_____　One has the boat; the other has the money.

---

6. What has four wheels and flies?

　　_____　A car.

　　_____　An airplane.

　　_____　A garbage truck.

7. What do termites do when they want to relax?

　　_____ Termites don't relax.

　　_____ They take a coffee table break.

　　_____ They take a nap.

8. How do you know that robbers are really strong?

　　_____ They lift weights.

　　_____ They take courses to improve their strength.

　　_____ They hold up banks.

9. Why are chefs mean?

　　_____ They beat the eggs and whip the cream.

　　_____ They stir the batter and knead the dough.

　　_____ They butter the bread and toast it.

10. Why did the man tiptoe past the medicine chest?

　　_____ He didn't want to wake the sleeping pills.

　　_____ He didn't want to wake his wife.

　　_____ The floor was cold.

11. What do you get if you cross an alley cat with a canary?

　　　_____　A cat that sings.

　　　_____　A peeping Tom.

　　　_____　A catastrophe.

12. What question can never be answered "yes"?

　　　_____　Are you a man?

　　　_____　Are you busy?

　　　_____　Are you asleep?

13. Why does he always wear a watch?

　　　_____　He likes to take his time.

　　　_____　He wants to know what time it is.

　　　_____　So he won't lose it.

14. Why are the floors of a basketball court always so damp?

　　　_____　The gym is next to the pool.

　　　_____　They are washed before the game.

　　　_____　The players dribble a lot.

15. How can you keep an elephant from charging?

    _____ You can't; just get out of his way.

    _____ Take away his credit cards.

    _____ Distract him.

---

16. When can a horse eat best?

    _____ When he doesn't have a bit in his mouth.

    _____ When he is hungry.

    _____ After 5:00 P.M.

---

17. Why shouldn't you take a leopard to the cleaners?

    _____ He will scare them.

    _____ They will remove his spots.

    _____ Leopards don't have anything to clean.

---

18. If you buy a fresh egg from a farm, how can you be sure that it doesn't have a chick in it?

    _____ Ask the farmer if it does.

    _____ Check another egg that the hen has hatched.

    _____ Buy a duck egg.

19. What is the difference between a flea and a cat?

　　　_____　A cat is large, and a flea is small.

　　　_____　A cat can have fleas, but a flea can't have cats.

　　　_____　A cat has whiskers and a tail, and a flea does not.

---

20. Why was the baseball player arrested?

　　　_____　They caught him stealing bases.

　　　_____　They found him with a stolen car.

　　　_____　He was caught drinking and driving.

---

21. What's the easiest way to catch a fish?

　　　_____　Use good bait.

　　　_____　Have someone throw you a fish.

　　　_____　Take fishing lessons.

---

22. What happened to the lady who swallowed a teaspoon?

　　　_____　She had to go to the hospital.

　　　_____　She couldn't stir.

　　　_____　She coughed it up.

Target Area 5 | **Completing**
Humor | **Jokes**

DIRECTIONS: Each joke has 3 possible endings. All the endings could fit, but only one of them is funny. Mark the ending which makes the sentence **funny.**

EXAMPLE: Old refrigerators never die, they just

_____ wear out.

_____ stop working.

__X__ lose their cool.

---

1. I know someone who likes arguing so much that he

   _____ can't keep any friends.

   _____ will argue with anyone.

   _____ won't eat anything that agrees with him.

---

2. My home town is so small that

   _____ it only has 50 people in it.

   _____ they close the library when someone takes out the book.

   _____ it only has one bank in it.

3. I eat my meals standing on one foot because

   _____ it is more comfortable than sitting.
   _____ I don't have a table.
   _____ I want to have a balanced diet.

---

4. Old mailmen never die, they just

   _____ work until they are 65.
   _____ lose their zip.
   _____ quit their route and take care of themselves.

---

5. My cellar is so damp that when I set a mousetrap

   _____ I don't catch anything.
   _____ I catch rats.
   _____ I catch fish.

---

6. The weakest animal in the world is the frog because

   _____ he will croak if you touch him.
   _____ he is so small.
   _____ his skin is very fragile.

7. My doctor put me on a seafood diet, and now I only eat when

    _____ I am hungry.

    _____ I see food.

    _____ it is mealtime.

---

8. My house is so old that the insurance for it covers fires

    _____ and Indian raids.

    _____ and floods.

    _____ and theft.

---

9. The best way to keep a skunk from smelling is to

    _____ stay away from it.

    _____ have it operated on.

    _____ hold its nose.

---

10. I know an artist who is so bad he can't even

    _____ finish a picture.

    _____ draw unemployment checks.

    _____ remember his name.

11. Did you hear about the man who drank eight Cokes and

    _____ 2 milkshakes?

    _____ burped 7-Up?

    _____ ate 4 hamburgers?

---

12. That girl is so shy that she goes into a closet to

    _____ change her mind.

    _____ pick out her clothes.

    _____ look for a friend.

---

13. My newest invention is a square bathtub that

    _____ squares can use.

    _____ never leaves a ring.

    _____ fits better in a corner.

---

14. Did you hear about the street cleaner who was fired because

    _____ he didn't do a good job?

    _____ he took too long a lunch hour?

    _____ he couldn't keep his mind in the gutter?

15. The best way to catch a squirrel is to

   _____ offer him nuts.

   _____ climb a tree.

   _____ climb a tree and act like a nut.

---

16. Did you hear about the woman who put a clock under her desk because she

   _____ wanted to work overtime?

   _____ didn't want to hear it ticking?

   _____ couldn't find anywhere else to put it?

---

17. I know a guy who wouldn't buy Christmas seals because

   _____ he was Jewish.

   _____ he didn't know what to feed them.

   _____ he was too cheap.

---

18. Mail service is so slow that my package of flower seeds

   _____ came as a bouquet.

   _____ got lost in the mail.

   _____ came three weeks late.

19. My eyes are so bad that when I was walking in the woods, I picked up a

   _____ stick to kill a snake.

   _____ snake to kill a stick.

   _____ rock to kill a snake.

20. I can tell my pet owl is sick because

   _____ he doesn't give a hoot.

   _____ he doesn't look well.

   _____ he's not eating.

21. Did you hear about the rich flea who

   _____ bought a bank?

   _____ made money on his investments?

   _____ bought his own dog?

22. A pig should never get sick because he would have to

   _____ take two aspirin and go to bed.

   _____ be killed before he is cured.

   _____ be kept away from the rest of the pigs.

23. I can tell this is a dogwood tree from its

   _____ trunk.

   _____ leaves.

   _____ bark.

24. There is a new doctor doll that you wind up and

   _____ it says "mama."

   _____ it operates on batteries.

   _____ nothing happens.

25. Did you hear about the cannibal who wanted to

   _____ stop where they serve truck drivers?

   _____ write a book?

   _____ go to the movies?

26. Did you hear about the composer who took so many baths that he

   _____ got wrinkled skin?

   _____ began writing soap operas?

   _____ changed professions?

27. My cough should sound better today, because I

　　_____　took some medicine for it.

　　_____　have had it for 2 weeks.

　　_____　practiced it all night.

28. Crime is so bad in my town that

　　_____　a thief moved to another city.

　　_____　a bank robber was mugged on the way to his getaway car.

　　_____　the statistics on criminals rose 20 percent.

29. A sure-fire way to double your money is to

　　_____　fold it.

　　_____　invest it.

　　_____　save it.

30. Did you hear about the secretary who came to work in a bathing suit because her boss told her

　　_____　the office was very warm?

　　_____　she was going to work in the secretarial pool?

　　_____　she had a nice figure?

**Target Area 5
Humor** | **Matching Definitions**

DIRECTIONS: These definitions are humorous. Choose the correct word from the list above each group of definitions, and write it on the line.

EXAMPLE: drizzle   rectangle

rectangle _____ the result of a head-on collision

drizzle _____ a thundercloud with a slow leak in it

---

1. bore   actor   criminal   taxi driver

   _____ someone who has nothing to say and says it

   _____ someone who drives away customers

   _____ someone who tries to be everything but himself

   _____ someone who gets caught

---

2. flea   silverfish   paradox   old-timer

   _____ two doctors

   _____ imitation goldfish

   _____ 75-year-old watch

   _____ bug that's gone to the dogs

3. real estate   margarine   ping-pong   rebate

_____ put another worm on a hook

_____ butter from an imitation cow

_____ something that proves dirt isn't cheap

_____ miniature tennis

---

4. mustache   desk   graham cracker   fireproof

_____ relatives of the boss

_____ misplaced eyebrow

_____ type of metric cookie

_____ garbage dump with drawers

---

5. zebra   lawsuit   medicine ball   toupee

_____ garment worn by policemen

_____ dance for sick people

_____ a horse behind bars

_____ ear-to-ear carpeting

6. protein   handicap   wholesale   warehouse

_____ in favor of teenagers

_____ what you say when you are lost

_____ where a gopher goes to buy a new house

_____ a hat that is easy to find

Target Area 5 | Rewriting
Humor | Puns

DIRECTIONS: The underlined word in each sentence **sounds like** the words that fit in the sentence. Rewrite the sentence replacing the underlined word with the correct words.

EXAMPLE: The man wants to selfish for a living.

The man wants to sell fish for a living.

1. Whose car should we take, minor yours?

2. Orange you going to eat some lunch?

3. Lettuce go to the store to buy some food.

4. A cadillac mean if you pull on its tail.

5. This is a <u>bigotry</u> than that tree.

6. I <u>avenue</u> chair in the living room.

7. <u>Canoe</u> get me a glass of milk while you are up?

8. Would you like to sit on <u>deceit</u> or the stool?

9. <u>Dishes</u> the worst food I have ever eaten.

10. I like that picture, how much does it <u>sulphur</u>?

11. I have <u>tulips</u> and one nose on my face.

12. It is fine <u>toboggan</u> for a good price at a flea market.

13. Who goes there, <u>manner</u> beast?

14. Plant the seed and let's see what will <u>turnip</u>.

15. Did your <u>antelope</u> or is she getting married in a church?

16. If you have <u>cashew</u> don't have to wait in line to pay.

17. It's hard to keep track of you. One <u>miniature</u> here and one <u>miniature</u> there.

18. The baby's <u>panther</u> wet, he needs to be changed.

19. It was an accident, I didn't <u>planet</u> this way.

20. We will <u>coincide</u> if it starts to rain.

21. I invited her to dinner; I hope you <u>lacquer</u>.

22. Why are you coming <u>insulate</u> when you said you'd be early?

Target Area 5
Humor

Understanding Word Drawings

DIRECTIONS: Each group of letters represents a familiar word or phrase. The way the letters are arranged on the page is important. It shows what the word or phrase is. When you have decided what word or phrase each group of letters represents, write it on the line.
HINT: An answer key for this exercise is on page 255; the answers **are not in order.**

EXAMPLE: E R I F *backfire*

C
C
I
H

1. _____

S
T
A
I
R
S

2. _____

MIND
MATTER

3. _____

VISION
VISION

4. _____

ENGAGE   MENT

5. _____

SEC
OND

6. _____

Y
R
R
U
H

7. _____

```
DANCE
A       C
N       N
C       A
ECNAD
```

8. _____

MAN
BOARD

9. _____

LEAF
LEAF
LEAF   CLOVER
LEAF

10. _____

STA   TION

11. _____

P_pO_pD

12. _____

talk

13. _____

R|E|A|D

14. _____

R
O
RAIL
D

15. _____

E Z
iiiiiiiii

16. _____

SIGN
....

17. _____

```
        E
        L      SAFETY
        K      SAFETY
        C      SAFETY
        U      SAFETY
        B
```

18. _____

GREEN   N V

19. _____

✓✓ ✓
COUNTER

20. _____

_____ ✓

21. _____

BANANA ←
BANANA

22. _____

HE'S   HIMSELF

23. _____

DO   ft.   OR

24. _____

ANSWER KEY

2 peas in a pod	buckle up for safety
top banana	square dance
four-leaf clover	split second
broken engagement	man overboard
small talk	railroad crossing
check-out counter	blank check
easy on the eyes	double vision
mind over matter	station break
read between the lines	foot in the door
hiccup	sign on the dotted line
he's beside himself	hurry up
downstairs	green with envy

Target Area 6
NUMBERS/SYMBOLS

Target Area 6
Numbers/Symbols | Matching Symbols and Words

DIRECTIONS: Draw a line from each symbol to the word it stands for.

EXAMPLE:

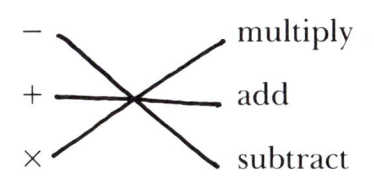

− multiply
+ add
× subtract

¢	equals	@	and
%	percent	i.e.	copyright
÷	dollar	etc.	that is
=	cent	©	at
$	divide	&	et cetera

▲	circle	✓	number
■	triangle	*	arrow
●	rectangle	#	cross
▬	oval	+	asterisk
⬭	square	→	check

♦	hearts	?	brackets
♣	diamonds	[ ]	degree
♥	spades	,	question mark
♠	clubs	!	comma
		°	exclamation point

259

🚫P	school crossing
🚗💨 (slippery car diamond)	 no parking
⊗	 slippery when wet
🏠 (children in house)	 railroad crossing

---

🚭	handicapped access
♿	 public telephone
🚺	 women's washroom
☎	 no smoking

Target Area 6
Numbers/Symbols | Matching Numbers and Facts

DIRECTIONS: Draw a line from each number to the word that is associated with it.

EXAMPLE:

2 — quartet
4 — duet
(lines crossed)

12	trio	2	octet
3	decade	8	quintet
2	dozen	5	duet
10	pair	6	sextet
12	feet in a yard	1	double
5280	inches in a foot	2	triple
36	inches in a yard	3	single
3	feet in a mile	4	quadruple
24	minutes in $\frac{1}{2}$ hour	1	to go
60	hours in day	2	for the money
30	seconds in minute	3	to get ready
40	hours in work week	4	for the show

14	Christmas
4	Valentine's Day
25	Independence Day
1	April Fool's Day

4	suits in a deck
52	cards in a deck
13	cards in a suit
3	face cards in a suit

16	teaspoons in a tablespoon
2	pints in a quart
4	quarts in a gallon
3	ounces in a pound

1969	man first lands on the moon
1492	Columbus discovers America
1976	Bicentennial year
1946	end of World War II

3	innings in baseball
6	periods in hockey
9	points for a touchdown
2	points for a basket

360	degrees in a circle
212	normal temperature
32	boiling point
98.6	freezing point

12	weeks in a year
52	days in a year
100	years in a century
365	months in a year

8	sides in a triangle
4	sides in a square
3	sides in a pentagon
5	sides in an octagon

Target Area 6
Numbers/Symbols

Identifying Numbers from Descriptions

DIRECTIONS: Write the number that the words describe.

EXAMPLE: number of eyes you have __2__

1. number of tires on a car _____

2. a number before 16 _____

3. number considered unlucky _____

4. number of years in a century minus 1 _____

5. the voting age _____

6. number of commandments _____

7. number of wheels on a tricycle _____

8. number of toes on 1 foot _____

9. the number before 12 _____

10. players on a baseball team _____

11. number that looks like an upside down 9 _____

12. number of lives a cat has _____

13. number of pounds in a ton _____

14. number of days in September _____

15. number of nickels in a quarter _____

16. number in a pair _____

17. cost of an air mail stamp _____

18. mandatory retirement age _____

19. years in a presidential term _____

20. legal driving age in your state _____

21. number of letters in the alphabet _____

22. number of letters in your last name _____

23. number of rooms in your home _____

Target Area 6
Numbers/Symbols

Answering Questions about Quantities

DIRECTIONS: Write the number that answers the question.

EXAMPLE: How many pennies in a nickel? __5__

1. How many nickels in a dime? _____

2. How many nickels in a quarter? _____

3. How many dimes in a half dollar? _____

4. How many nickels in 35¢? _____

5. How many quarters in a dollar? _____

6. How many pennies in a quarter? _____

7. How many nickels in a half dollar? _____

8. How many dimes in a dollar? _____

9. How many quarters in a half dollar? _____

10. How many nickels in a dollar? _____

11. How many nickels in 65¢? _____

12. How many dimes in $2.00? _____

13. How many quarters in $1.50? _____

14. How many half dollars in $5.00? _____

15. How many pennies in a dollar? _____

16. How many dimes in 70¢? _____

17. How many inches in 2 feet? _____

18. How many eggs in a half dozen? _____

19. How many inches in a yard? _____

20. How many seconds in a half minute? _____

21. How many minutes in a half hour? _____

22. How many shoes in 2 pairs? _____

23. How many cupcakes in 2 dozen? _____

24. How many minutes in an hour and a half? _____

25. How many hours in 2 days? _____

26. How many feet in 2 yards? _____

27. How many inches in 5 feet? _____

28. How many ounces in half a pound? _____

29. How many halves in a whole? _____

30. How many minutes in a quarter hour? _____

Target Area 6 Numbers/Symbols | Adding Amounts of Money

DIRECTIONS: Add the amounts in each item and write the total.

EXAMPLE: 7 quarters $1.75

1. 4 nickels, 4 pennies _____

2. 2 nickels, 1 dime, 8 pennies _____

3. 2 dimes, 2 quarters, 1 penny _____

4. 7 nickels, 1 dime, 6 pennies _____

5. 4 dimes, 5 nickels, 2 pennies _____

6. 2 quarters, 3 nickels, 1 dime _____

7. 8 pennies, 2 nickels, 3 dimes, 1 quarter _____

8. 3 quarters, 1 nickel, 2 pennies _____

9. 18 pennies, 1 nickel, 1 dime _____

10. 1 half dollar, 3 nickels, 4 pennies _____

11. 3 quarters, 3 dimes, 1 nickel, 2 pennies _____

12. 6 dimes, 6 nickels, 6 pennies _____

13. 3 quarters, 4 dimes, 1 nickel, 2 pennies _____

14. 8 dimes, 6 nickels, 2 quarters _____

15. 3 dollars, 3 half dollars, 3 dimes _____

16. 17 pennies, 2 dimes, 1 quarter, 2 nickels _____

17. 1 penny, 1 dollar, 1 quarter _____

18. 2 dimes, 4 quarters, 3 pennies _____

19. 1 half dollar, 3 quarters, 3 dimes _____

20. 6 dimes, 6 quarters _____

21. 3 pennies, 2 quarters, 6 nickels _____

22. 5 dimes, 1 quarter, 10 pennies, 3 nickels _____

23. 5 half dollars, 2 quarters _____

Target Area 6
Numbers/Symbols | Ranking Costs

DIRECTIONS: Rank the items in each list from the least expensive (**1**) to the most expensive (**3**). Write the number on the line next to each item.

EXAMPLE: _3_ motor home
         _2_ tent
         _1_ air mattress

1. ___ apple
   ___ motorcycle
   ___ basketball

2. ___ diamond ring
   ___ dozen eggs
   ___ pencil

3. ___ house
   ___ piano
   ___ new car

4. ___ cheeseburger
   ___ coke
   ___ french fries

5. ___ washing machine
   ___ toaster
   ___ microwave

6. ___ black-and-white TV
   ___ transistor radio
   ___ stereo set

7. ____ pair of socks
   ____ pair of shoes
   ____ pair of skis

8. ____ daily paper
   ____ Time Magazine
   ____ Sunday paper

9. ____ typewriter
   ____ typing paper
   ____ desk

10. ____ renting a yacht
    ____ renting a canoe
    ____ renting a car

11. ____ 4 tires
    ____ 2 license plates
    ____ an automobile

12. ____ 6 magazines
    ____ 4 rakes
    ____ 2 wool coats

13. ____ tablecloth
    ____ table
    ____ washcloth

14. ____ mattress
    ____ blanket
    ____ pillow

15. ____ greeting card
    ____ stamp
    ____ dozen stamps

16. ____ movie ticket
    ____ airline ticket
    ____ traffic ticket

17. ____ transistor radio
    ____ portable tape recorder
    ____ color TV

18. ____ gallon of paint
    ____ gallon of milk
    ____ gallon of water

19. ____ dozen roses
    ____ dozen eggs
    ____ dozen doughnuts

20. ____ pound of butter
    ____ pound of salt
    ____ pound of shrimp

21. ____ jar of peanut butter
    ____ jar of caviar
    ____ jar of baby food

22. ____ footstool
    ____ rocking chair
    ____ couch

23. ____ floor lamp
    ____ candle
    ____ flashlight

24. ____ 3 nails
    ____ 2 hammers
    ____ 1 cord of wood

Target Area 6
Numbers/Symbols | Identifying Equivalent Values

DIRECTIONS: There are 6 amounts described in each item. Underline all the amounts which are the same. **HINT**: there are at least 3 amounts that are the same for each question.

EXAMPLE: 8 nickels   15¢   <u>20¢</u>

23¢   <u>2 dimes</u>   <u>$\frac{1}{2}$ of 40</u>

---

1. $\frac{1}{2}$ of 10   3 pennies   1 nickel

   days in week   5 $\frac{1}{4}$ of 20

---

2. 3 feet $\frac{1}{2}$ of 6 feet   36 inches

   36 ounces   1 yard   1 cord

---

3. 21   26   48 ÷ 2

   2 dozen   1 less than 25   inches in 2 ft.

---

4. yrs. in century   500 $\frac{1}{2}$ of 200

   100   200   10 decades

---

5. 1 quarter   2 decades   2 nickels

   2 dozen + 1 $\frac{1}{2}$ of 50   1/4 century

6. number in trio | number in pair | 1/4 of 10
   $\frac{1}{2}$ of 4 | pints in a quart | 4

7. 3 more than 5 | a quartet | 2 less than 10
   $\frac{1}{2}$ of 16 | 4 pairs | $\frac{1}{2}$ dozen

8. 3 quarters | 45¢ | 2 quarters
   4 dimes | 9 nickels | $\frac{1}{2}$ of 90

9. 3 more than 10 | 1 dozen + 1 | 12
   3 × 5 | 1 dime + 1 penny | 13

10. $\frac{1}{2}$ of 24 | 1 penny + 1 dime | inches in foot
    1 dime + 1 nickel | 1 dozen | 12

11. 1 half dollar | 2 quarters | 2-dollar bill
    60 pennies | 5 dimes | 10 nickels

12. 1 less than 16 | 3 more than 11 | a dozen
    1 dime + 1 nickel | 15 pennies | $\frac{1}{2}$ of 25

Target Area 6
Numbers/Symbols | Completing Numbers in a Series

DIRECTIONS: Each group of numbers follows a pattern. Figure out what the pattern is, and then write the next two numbers in that pattern on the lines provided.

EXAMPLE: 8, 10   12, 14   16, 18   _20_, _22_

---

1. 10, 11   20, 21   30, 31   _____, _____

---

2. 5, 10   15, 20   25, 30   _____, _____

---

3. 21, 20   19, 18   17, 16   _____, _____

---

4. 8, 1   6, 1   4, 1   _____, _____

---

5. 1, 0   2, 1   3, 2   _____, _____

---

6. 25, 30   35, 40   45, 50   _____, _____

7. 99, 98   88, 87   77, 76   ____, ____

8. 5, 5   6, 6   7, 7   ____, ____

9. 0, 2   0, 4   0, 6   ____, ____

10. 68, 60   58, 50   48, 40   ____, ____

11. 21, 19   17, 15   13, 11   ____, ____

12. 99, 96   93, 90   87, 84   ____, ____

13. 1, 10   10, 100   100, 1000   ____, ____

14. 5, 10   6, 12   7, 14   ____, ____

15. 3, 30   4, 40   5, 50   ____, ____

16. 9, 6   8, 7   7, 8   ____, ____

17. 100, 10   90, 9   80, 8   ____, ____

18. 230, 231   232, 233   234, 235   ____, ____

19. 1, $1\frac{1}{2}$ 3, $3\frac{1}{2}$ 5, $5\frac{1}{2}$ ____, ____

20. 80, 40   40, 20   20, 10   ____, ____

Target Area 6
Numbers/Symbols

Correcting Numbers In a Series

DIRECTIONS: There are 5 numbers on each line. 4 of the numbers are related and follow a pattern. One number does not belong with the others in the sequence. Cross it out. **HINT**: when the incorrect number is crossed out, the remaining numbers should be related and follow each other in a series.

EXAMPLE: 1   2   3   ~~5~~   4

---

1. 1985   1984   1872   1983   1982

---

2. 10   60   20   30   40

---

3. 11   22   33   32   44

---

4. 2   4   8   6   16

---

5. 80   40   20   10   2

---

6. 3   8   10   13   18

7. 4   60   600   6,000   60,000

8. 50   44   45   40   35

9. 7   70   8   80   6

10. 79   81   73   83   85

11. 6   12   18   20   24

12. 87   74   77   67   57

13. 101   202   303   404   202

14. 2,300   2,298   2,299   2,296   2,294

15. 45,321   4,321   321   21   1

16.	56565	65656	56565	66566	65656
17.	13333	33333	31333	33133	33313
18.	491	440	194	941	149
19.	36	47	58	60	69
20.	8	9	17	25	33

Target Area 6 Numbers/Symbols | Solving Arithmetic Problems

DIRECTIONS: Complete the missing parts of each problem.

EXAMPLE: $2 \times 4 =$ <u>8</u> $+ 1 =$ <u>9</u>

1. $3 + 7 =$ ______ $+ 4 =$ ______ $- 3 =$ ______

2. $25 + 5 =$ ______ $\div 2 =$ ______ $+ 1 =$ ______

3. $4 + 9 =$ ______ $+ 2 =$ ______ $+ 3 =$ ______

4. $15 + 4 =$ ______ $- 1 =$ ______ $\div 3 =$ ______

5. $10 + 7 =$ ______ $+ 3 =$ ______ $- 6 =$ ______

6. $3 \times 7 =$ ______ $+ 4 =$ ______ $\div 5 =$ ______

7. $35 \div 5 =$ ______ $+ 1 =$ ______ $\times 2 =$ ______

8. 16 + 6 = _____ + 7 = _____ − 6 = _____

9. 30 + 2 = _____ ÷ 4 = _____ + 5 = _____

10. 6 + 11 = _____ + 5 = _____ + 4 = _____

11. 42 − 3 = _____ − 6 = _____ − 4 = _____

12. 6 × 7 = _____ + 3 = _____ ÷ 9 = _____

13. 36 ÷ 6 = _____ × 4 = _____ + 1 = _____

14. 11 + 8 = _____ + 7 = _____ + 7 = _____

15. 40 ÷ 5 = _____ × 3 = _____ + 4 = _____

16. 15 + 11 = _____ + 4 = _____ ÷ 5 = _____

17. 16 + 4 = _____ − 9 = _____ − 3 = _____

18. 50 ÷ 25 = _____ × 12 = _____ + 8 = _____

19. 31 + 7 = _____ + 7 = _____ ÷ 5 = _____

20. 4 × 4 = _____ + 6 = _____ ÷ 2 = _____

21. 47 − 6 = _____ − 8 = _____ − 3 = _____

22. 20 × 3 = _____ − 7 = _____ − 4 = _____

23. 12 × 3 = _____ + 3 = _____ ÷ 3 = _____

24. 55 ÷ 5 = _____ − 4 = _____ × 7 = _____

Target Area 6
Numbers/Symbols

Solving Multi-Step Computations

DIRECTIONS: Read the instructions and do as they say. Write your answer on the line. Use the blank space on the right to do your figuring if you need to.

EXAMPLE: Start with 10.

Add 9 ___*19*___

Subtract 3 ___*16*___   Answer: 16

---

1. Start with 3.

   Multiply by 2 _____

   Add 8 _____

   Subtract 3 _____   Answer: 11

---

2. Start with 7.

   Add 3 _____

   Multiply by 3 _____

   Divide by 6 _____   Answer: 5

3. Start with 25.

   Double it _____

   Divide by 5 _____

   Subtract 3 _____

   Multiply by 4 _____   Answer: 28

---

4. Start with 10.

   Add 8 _____

   Add 5 _____

   Add 2 _____

   Multiply by 2 _____   Answer: 50

---

5. Start with 6.

   Subtract 2 _____

   Multiply by 4 _____

   Add 5 _____

   Subtract 7 _____   Answer: 14

6. Start with 13.

   Subtract 7 _____

   Multiply by 8 _____

   Add 2 _____

   Double it _____   Answer: 100

---

7. Start with 19.

   Add 1 _____

   Multiply by 4 _____

   Divide by 8 _____

   Add 3 _____   Answer: 13

---

8. Start with 16.

   Divide by 2 _____

   Add 1 _____

   Multiply by 8 _____

   Add 4 _____   Answer: 76

9. Start with 31.

   Subtract 6 _____

   Multiply by 4 _____

   Subtract 7 _____

   Subtract 2 _____ Answer: 91

---

10. Start with 40.

    Divide by 10 _____

    Multiply by 7 _____

    Add 2 _____

    Multiply by 2 _____ Answer: 60

---

11. Start with 3.

    Multiply by 9 _____

    Subtract 5 _____

    Subtract 7 _____

    Multiply by 2 _____

    Add 6 _____ Answer: 36

12. Start with 9

   Add 8 _____

   Add 6 _____

   Add 9 _____

   Add 5 _____

   Add 4 _____   Answer: 41

---

13. Start with 8.

   Multiply by 7 _____

   Add 4 _____

   Subtract 8 _____

   Subtract 2 _____

   Multiply by 3 _____   Answer: 150

14. Start with 17.

    Add 8 _____

    Multiply by 3 _____

    Subtract 6 _____

    Subtract 7 _____

    Subtract 4 _____   Answer: 58

---

15. Start with 5.

    Multiply by 11 _____

    Subtract 8 _____

    Subtract 2 _____

    Divide by 3 _____

    Subtract 2 _____   Answer: 13

16. Start with 4.

   Add 3 _____

   Double it _____

   Add 4 _____

   Subtract 7 _____

   Subtract 10 _____   Answer: 1

---

17. Start with 82.

   Subtract 6 _____

   Add 9 _____

   Add 5 _____

   Divide by 3 _____

   Double it _____   Answer: 60

18. Start with 70.

　　Subtract 7 _____

　　Subtract 6 _____

　　Subtract 12 _____

　　Divide by 9 _____

　　Double it _____   Answer: 10

---

19. Start with 2.

　　Multiply by 11 _____

　　Multiply by 2 _____

　　Add 6 _____

　　Divide by 5 _____

　　Multiply by 10 _____

　　Subtract 2 _____   Answer: 98

Target Area 6
Numbers/Symbols
Solving Math Story Problems

DIRECTIONS: Read each problem, figure out the answer, and write it on the line.

EXAMPLE: One lightbulb costs $1.20. How much would 3 cost? $3.60

1. If oranges are 3 for $1.00 and you buy a dozen, how much will they cost? _____

2. If the bill is $8.95 and you give the cashier $10.00, how much change will you get? _____

3. How much is a 10% tax on $58.00? _____

4. If a car gets 20 miles to the gallon of gas, how many miles can I go on 8 gallons? _____

5. If I weighed 210 pounds and then I lost 14 pounds, how much would I weigh? _____

6. How many feet is 4 yards of carpet? _____

7. How many 20¢ stamps can you buy with $1.00? _____

8. Pure gold is 24-carat gold. If you buy something that is 12-carat gold, what percentage is really gold? _____

9. Let's say I will be taking these people out to dinner: my wife and me, and our 2 sons and their wives. Each son has 2 children. I should make a reservation for how many people? _____

10. If you get up at 6:30 and must leave for work at 8:15, how much time do you have to get ready? _____

11. If you play 4 hands of bridge and each hand lasts 20 minutes, how much time did you spend playing bridge? _____

12. If you work 30 hours per week at a job, how many hours do you work in 3 weeks? _____

13. In 5 years a man will be 65. His wife is 7 years younger than he is. How old is she now? _____

14. If you buy ketchup for $1.15, mustard for 89 cents, hot dogs for $2.32, buns for 73 cents, and 2 liters of coke at $1.69 a liter, how much is your bill? _____

15. If it is 3:20 and you want to set an alarm to wake you in 45 minutes, what time should you set it for? _____

16. If you have lunch with 3 other people and receive one check for $18.00, how much would each of you owe if you divided it equally? _____

How much tip would you leave? _____

17. If today is March 15 and you need to make a doctor's appointment in exactly 2 weeks, what date would you make it for? _____

18. If you are mailing a package and the postage costs $1.19, the insurance costs $2.83, and you hand the clerk a five-dollar bill, how much change will you get? _____

    How many stamps can you buy with the change? _____

19. If a $20.00 item is on sale at 20% off, how much will it cost?
    _____

20. How much would you give as a 15% tip on a bill for $5.00?
    _____

21. Wallpaper comes in 27-inch-wide strips. How many full strips could be pasted on a wall 10 feet long? _____

    How many inches will be left over? _____

22. If I have an appointment at 3:00, and it takes me 40 minutes to get there, and I leave 15 minutes later than I should, what time will I get to the appointment? _____

23. If I am playing cards with 3 other people and I deal out the entire deck, how many cards will we each get? _____

24. If I am serving dinner to 8 people and using a recipe that calls for $\frac{1}{3}$ pound of chicken per person, how much chicken should I buy?

25. Let's say I have 230 pennies that I want to put in rolls. Each roll holds 50 pennies. How many rolls will I need? _____

Susan Howell Brubaker is Coordinator of Aphasia Rehabilitation at William Beaumont Hospital, Royal Oak, Michigan. The Speech and Language Pathology Department at Beaumont is accredited by the ASHA Professional Services Board. The author works exclusively with adults who have suffered communicative loss as a result of neurological dysfunction. She holds the B.S. from St. Lawrence University, Canton, N.Y., the M.S. from Ithaca College, Ithaca, N.Y., and the Certificate of Clinical Competence from the American Speech-Language-Hearing Association.

The manuscript was edited by Jean Owen. The book was designed by Elizabeth Hanson. The typeface for the text is Baskerville, based on an original design by John Baskerville in the eighteenth century, and the display face is Univers, designed by Adrian Frutiger about 1957. The book is printed on 60 lb. Springhill text paper and bound in GBC .035 gauge polyethelene Gebex covers and surelox plastic combs.

Manufactured in the United States of America.

ORDER FORM

To: WAYNE STATE UNIVERSITY PRESS
   The Leonard N. Simons Building
   5959 Woodward Avenue
   Detroit, Michigan 48202

Please send _____ copy/ies of Brubaker, *Workbook for Reasoning Skills* @ $25.00

_____ copy/ies of Brubaker, *Workbook for Language Skills* @ $25.00

_____ copy/ies of Brubaker, *Workbook for Aphasia* @ $10.95

_____ copy/ies of Brubaker, *Sourcebook for Aphasia* @ $12.00

_____ copy/ies of Wulf, *Aphasia, My World Alone* @ $9.50

Name _____

Institution _____

Address _____

City _____ State _____ Zip _____

_____ Check or money order enclosed. Add $1.00 for postage and handling.

_____ Charge to my MasterCard ☐ or Visa ☐

Acct. No. _____

Bank. No. (M/C) _____ Exp. Date _____

Michigan residents add 4% sales tax.

Direct phone orders to (313) 577-4603.